THE
NANTICOKE

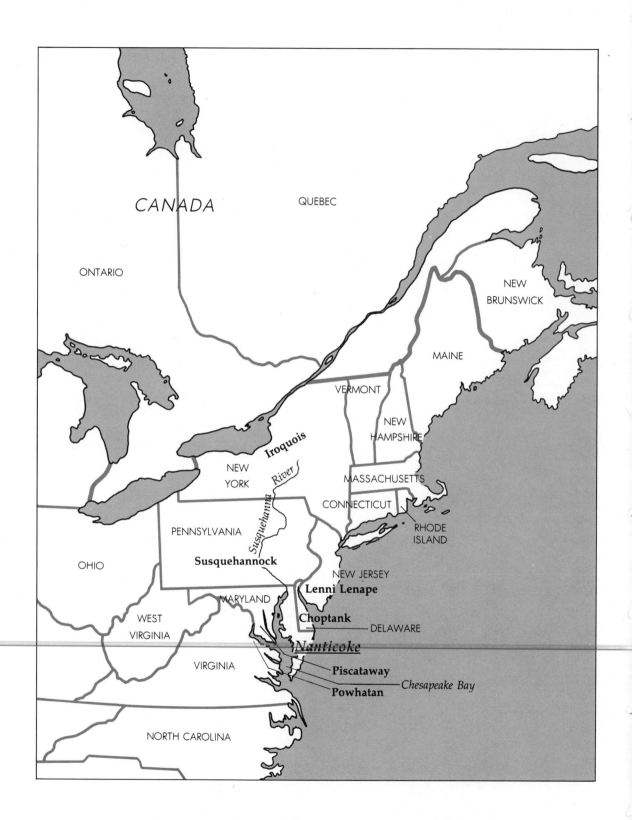

INDIANS OF NORTH AMERICA

THE
NANTICOKE

Frank W. Porter III

Director, Chelsea House Foundation
for American Indian Studies

CHELSEA HOUSE PUBLISHERS

New York   New Haven   Philadelphia

On the cover   A Nanticoke corn-shelling mortar.

Editor-in-Chief   Nancy Toff
Executive Editor   Remmel T. Nunn
Managing Editor   Karyn Gullen Browne
Copy Chief   Perry Scott King
Art Director   Giannella Garrett
Picture Editor   Elizabeth Terhune

Staff for THE NANTICOKE

Senior Editor   Marjorie P. K. Weiser
Senior Designer   Laurie Jewell
Design Assistant   Laura Lang
Copy Editors   Sean Dolan, Gillian Bucky
Picture Research   Susan B. Hamburger, Susan B. Popkin
Production Coordinator   Alma Rodriguez

Creative Director   Harold Steinberg

First printing

Library of Congress Cataloging-in-Publication Data

Porter, Frank W., 1947–
The Nanticoke.

(Indians of North America)
Bibliography: p.
Includes index.
1. Nanticoke Indians.   I. Title.   II. Series:
Indians of North America (Chelsea House Publishers)
E99.N14P67   1987   973'.0497   86-31775

ISBN 1-55546-686-9

CONTENTS

INDIANS OF NORTH AMERICA

CHELSEA HOUSE PUBLISHERS

INDIANS OF NORTH AMERICA: CONFLICT AND SURVIVAL

Frank W. Porter III

*The Indians survived our
open intention of wiping them
out, and since the tide turned
they have even weathered
our good intentions toward them,
which can be much more deadly.*

John Steinbeck
America and Americans

When Europeans first reached the North American continent, they found hundreds of tribes occupying a vast and rich country. The newcomers quickly recognized the wealth of natural resources. They were not, however, so quick or willing to recognize the spiritual, cultural, and intellectual riches of the people they called Indians.

The Indians of North America examines the problems that develop when people with different cultures come together. For American Indians, the consequences of their interaction with non-Indian people have been both productive and tragic. The Europeans believed they had "discovered" a "New World," but their religious bigotry, cultural bias, and materialistic world view kept them from appreciating and understanding the people who lived in it. All too often they attempted to change the way of life of the indigenous people. The Spanish conquistadores wanted the Indians as a source of labor. The Christian missionaries, many of whom were English, viewed them as potential converts. French traders and trappers used the Indians as a means to obtain pelts. As Francis Parkman, the 19th-century historian, stated, "Spanish civilization crushed the Indian; English civilization scorned and neglected him; French civilization embraced and cherished him."

Nearly 500 years later, many people think of American Indians as curious vestiges of a distant past, waging a futile war to survive in a Space Age society. Even today, our understanding of the history and culture of American Indians is too often derived from unsympathetic, culturally biased, and inaccurate reports. The American Indian, described and portrayed in thousands of movies, television programs, books, articles, and government studies, has either been raised to the status of the "noble savage" or disparaged as the "wild Indian" who resisted the westward expansion of the American frontier.

Where in this popular view are the real Indians, the human beings and communities whose ancestors can be traced back to ice-age hunters? Where are the creative and indomitable people whose sophisticated technologies used the natural resources to ensure their survival, whose military skill might even have prevented European settlement of North America if not for devastating epidemics and the disruption of the ecology? Where are the men and women who are today diligently struggling to assert their legal rights and express once again the value of their heritage?

The various Indian tribes of North America, like people everywhere, have a history that includes population expansion, adaptation to a range of regional environments, trade across wide networks, internal strife, and warfare. This was the reality. Europeans justified their conquests, however, by creating a mythical image of the New World and its native people. In this myth, the New World was a virgin land, waiting for the Europeans. The arrival of Christopher Columbus ended a timeless primitiveness for the original inhabitants.

Also part of this myth was the debate over the origins of the American Indians. Fantastic and diverse answers were proposed by the early explorers, missionaries, and settlers. Some thought that the Indians were descended from the Ten Lost Tribes of Israel, others that they were descended from inhabitants of the lost continent of Atlantis. One writer suggested that the Indians had reached North America in another Noah's ark.

A later myth, perpetrated by many historians, focused on the relentless persecution during the past five centuries until only a scattering of these "primitive" people remained to be herded onto reservations. This view fails to chronicle the overt and covert ways in which the Indians successfully coped with the intruders.

All of these myths presented one-sided interpretations that ignored the complexity of European and American events and policies. All left serious questions unanswered. What were the origins of the American Indians? Where did they come from? How and when did they get to the New World? What was their life—their culture—really like?

In the late 1800s, anthropologists and archaeologists in the Smithsonian Institution's newly created Bureau of American Ethnology in Washington, D. C., began to study scientifically the history and culture of the Indians of North America. They were motivated by an honest belief that the Indians were on the verge of extinction and that along with them would vanish their languages, religious beliefs, technology, myths, and legends. These men and women went out to visit, study, and record data from as many Indian communities as possible before this information was forever lost.

By this time there was a new myth in the national consciousness. American Indians existed as figures in the American past. They had performed a historical mission. They had challenged white settlers who trekked across the continent. Once conquered, however, they were supposed to accept graciously the way of life of their conquerors.

The reality again was different. American Indians resisted both actively and passively. They refused to lose their unique identity, to be assimilated into white society. Many whites viewed the Indians not only as members of a conquered nation but also as "inferior" and "unequal." The rights of the Indians could be expanded, contracted, or modified as the conquerors saw fit. In every generation, white society asked itself what to do with the American Indians. Their answers have resulted in the twists and turns of federal Indian policy.

There were two general approaches. One way was to raise the Indians to a "higher level" by "civilizing" them. Zealous missionaries considered it their Christian duty to elevate the Indian through conversion and scanty education. The other approach was to ignore the Indians until they disappeared under pressure from the ever-expanding white society. The myth of the "vanishing Indian" gave stronger support to the latter option, helping to justify the taking of the Indians' land.

Prior to the end of the 18th century, there was no national policy on Indians simply because the American nation had not yet come into existence. American Indians similarly did not possess a political or social unity with which to confront the various Europeans. They were not homogeneous. Rather, they were loosely formed bands and tribes, speaking nearly 300 languages and thousands of dialects. The collective identity felt by Indians today is a result of their common experiences of defeat and/or mistreatment at the hands of whites.

During the colonial period, the British crown did not have a coordinated policy toward the Indians of North America. Specific tribes (most notably the Iroquois and the Cherokee) became military and political pawns used by both the crown and the individual colonies. The success of the American Revolution brought no immediate change. When the United States acquired new territory from France and Mexico in the early 19th century, the federal government wanted to open this land to settlement by homesteaders. But the Indian tribes that lived on this land had signed treaties with European governments assuring their title to the land. Now the United States assumed legal responsibility for honoring these treaties.

At first, President Thomas Jefferson believed that the Louisiana Purchase contained sufficient land for both the Indians and the white population.

Within a generation, though, it became clear that the Indians would not be allowed to remain. In the 1830s the federal government began to coerce the eastern tribes to sign treaties agreeing to relinquish their ancestral land and move west of the Mississippi River. Whenever these negotiations failed, President Andrew Jackson used the military to remove the Indians. The southeastern tribes, promised food and transportation during their removal to the West, were instead forced to walk the "Trail of Tears." More than 4,000 men, women, and children died during this forced march. The "removal policy" was successful in opening the land to homesteaders, but it created enormous hardships for the Indians.

By 1871 most of the tribes in the United States had signed treaties ceding most or all of their ancestral land in exchange for reservations and welfare. The treaty terms were intended to bind both parties for all time. But in the General Allotment Act of 1887, the federal government changed its policy again. Now the goal was to make tribal members into individual landowners and farmers, encouraging their absorption into white society. This policy was advantageous to whites who were eager to acquire Indian land, but it proved disastrous for the Indians. One hundred thirty-eight million acres of reservation land were subdivided into tracts of 160, 80, or as little as 40 acres, and allotted to tribe members on an individual basis. Land owned in this way was said to have "trust status" and could not be sold. But the surplus land—all Indian land not allotted to individuals— was opened (for sale) to white settlers. Ultimately, more than 90 million acres of land were taken from the Indians by legal and illegal means.

The resulting loss of land was a catastrophe for the Indians. It was necessary to make it illegal for Indians to sell their land to non-Indians. The Indian Reorganization Act of 1934 officially ended the allotment period. Tribes that voted to accept the provisions of this act were reorganized, and an effort was made to purchase land within preexisting reservations to restore an adequate land base.

Ten years later, in 1944, federal Indian policy again shifted. Now the federal government wanted to get out of the "Indian business." In 1953 an act of Congress named specific tribes whose trust status was to be ended "at the earliest possible time." This new law enabled the United States to end unilaterally, whether the Indians wished it or not, the special status that protected the land in Indian tribal reservations. In the 1950s federal Indian policy was to transfer federal responsibility and jurisdiction to state governments, encourage the physical relocation of Indian peoples from reservations to urban areas, and hasten the termination, or extinction, of tribes.

Between 1954 and 1962 Congress passed specific laws authorizing the termination of more than 100 tribal groups. The stated purpose of the termination policy was to ensure the full and complete integration of Indians into American society. However, there is a less benign way to interpret this legislation. Even as termination was being discussed in Congress, 133 separate bills were introduced to permit the transfer of trust land ownership from Indians to non-Indians.

With the Johnson administration in the 1960s the federal government began to reject termination. In the 1970s yet another Indian policy emerged. Known as "self-determination," it favored keeping the protective role of the federal government while increasing tribal participation in, and control of, important areas of local government. In 1983 President Reagan, in a policy statement on Indian affairs, restated the unique "government to government" relationship of the United States with the Indians. However, federal programs since then have moved toward transferring Indian affairs to individual states, which have long desired to gain control of Indian land and resources.

As long as American Indians retain power, land, and resources that are coveted by the states and the federal government, there will continue to be a "clash of cultures," and the issues will be contested in the courts, Congress, the White House, and even in the international human rights community. To give all Americans a greater comprehension of the issues and conflicts involving American Indians today is a major goal of this series. These issues are not easily understood, nor can these conflicts be readily resolved. The study of North American Indian history and culture is a necessary and important step toward that comprehension. All Americans must learn the history of the relations between the Indians and the federal government, recognize the unique legal status of the Indians, and understand the heritage and cultures of the Indians of North America.

*The Maryland settlers crossed the ocean in
two ships, the Ark and the Dove.*

FIRST MEETING
WITH
EUROPEANS

"We are driven back," the aged warrior said, "until we can retreat no further. Our hatchets are broken. Our bows are snapped. Our fires are nearly gone out. A little longer and the white man will cease to pursue us, for we shall cease to exist."

The year was 1853. The speaker represented the Nanticoke Indians, then living among the Iroquois on a reservation in Canada. These Nanticokes were petitioning the Maryland House of Delegates to receive payment for lands they had once possessed on the Eastern Shore of that state.

A committee had been appointed by the House of Delegates to study the Nanticokes' claim. Its members had thoroughly searched the available land records. They found that the state had legally acquired the Eastern Shore lands by paying the Nanticokes for it.

"Our forefathers and theirs parted friends," the committee reported, puzzled by the unexpected claim. "Until the recent appeal made by their descendants, it was thought by the people of Maryland that the tribe had ceased to exist." The report added, "In our own State, not one now remains to tell the tale of their former greatness."

At about the same time, however, across the Chesapeake Bay in Sussex County, Delaware, another group of Nanticokes was dealing with a different government body. Not all of the Nanticokes had moved north to Canada. Several families had stayed on the Eastern Shore. Among them were Levin Sockum, a landholder who owned and operated a general store in Sussex County, and his relatives.

Sockum was accused of violating a Delaware law that prohibited the sale or loan of firearms and accessories to a "Negro, mulatto, or person of color." Sockum had admitted to selling powder and shot to Isaac Harman, his son-in-law. The prosecuting attorney was trying to prove that Harman was indeed a mulatto, or person of mixed black and white descent. No witness could provide information about Harman's ancestors.

Finally, Lydia Clark was called to the witness stand. Clark, a blood relative of Harman, testified that before the American Revolution an Irish lady had purchased a slave who came from the Congo. Later she had married him. The children of this couple married with people of the Nanticoke tribe. Clark's testimony satisfied the court that Harman was indeed a mulatto, and Sockum was found guilty.

By the mid-19th century, when these two episodes took place, the Nanticoke Indians had lost many of their traditions along with their traditional homeland. Part of the tribe had left Maryland and moved to Canada. Another part of the tribe had stayed and were beginning a new life further to the east, in Delaware. Wherever they went, it seemed, laws made by newcomers were challenging their identity and their connections to their own past.

Europeans had first settled in the territory that is now Maryland and Delaware more than 200 years earlier. When they came, the land was inhabited by the Nanticoke as well as the Choptank, Piscataway, and some 40 other tribes. Each tribe was self-governing and functioned well in its environment. The Indians produced food by farming, as well as by hunting and collecting small animals and edible plants. They knew the rivers and forests of their country more intimately than any other people who have lived there since. The Indians of the Eastern Shore traded widely with other tribes, especially the Powhatan, the Susquehan-

nock, and the Iroquois, who lived in what are now Virginia, Pennsylvania, and New York.

Little is actually known about the first meetings between the Indians living on the Eastern Shore and the Europeans. It is known that in 1524 the Italian navigator Giovanni da Verrazano was in the area, exploring the coast of North America. Verrazano and his men kidnapped a young Indian boy and frightened his companions by firing guns over their heads. In 1572 Spanish Jesuit priests attempted to establish a mission in Virginia, but they were eventually murdered by the Indians. In 1608 Captain John Smith of Jamestown, Virginia, began to explore the rivers of Maryland. Some years later another Virginian, William Claiborne, became the first European to settle in what is now Maryland. In 1627 Claiborne opened a trading post on Kent Island in Chesapeake Bay.

The first recorded contact of the Nanticoke with Europeans involved Captain Smith. In 1608, while exploring Chesapeake Bay, he and his crew of 14 visited with a few smaller tribes on the lower Eastern Shore of Maryland. Then they sailed into the Kuskarawaok River. The Kuskarawaoks, later to be known as the Nanticoke Indians, appeared along the shore of the river. Some perched in trees, which they had climbed in order to get a better view of the approaching strangers. In the villages Smith and his men had previously visited, they had been received with hospitality. The Nanticoke, however, began to shoot arrows at the boat while it was still some distance away. The arrows fell short. Prudently, the English anchored in the middle of the river.

Despite several attempts, Smith was unable to convince the Nanticoke of his friendly intentions. After a long and tense night on board, the explorers awoke to an unusual scene on the shore. The Nanticoke seemed to have ended their attack. They were carrying baskets, which appeared to be filled with food. Smith, wary of Indians bearing gifts, ordered his men to fire their muskets over the heads of the Indians. Frightened by the blast of the guns, the Nanticoke dropped their baskets and fled into the reeds along the bank of the river. Only then did the English notice warriors hiding in the reeds, ready to ambush them if they had gone ashore.

That afternoon Smith ordered his men to row closer to the shore. The Indians were nowhere to be seen. Near the abandoned baskets, however, were small pools of blood, showing that some of the Nanticoke had been wounded by the muskets.

On the opposite shore of the river, Smith discovered some Indian huts. Fires were still burning in the hearths, but no person could be found. Smith left some glass beads, bells, pieces of copper, and looking glasses as tokens of friendship for the Indians to find on their return. He then sailed back to the bay, anchoring for the night.

In the morning, four Indians who had been fishing approached the English boat in their canoe. Smith per-

Captain John Smith

William Claiborne, a Virginia colonist, became the first European to settle in what is now Maryland when he opened this trading post on Kent Island in Chesapeake Bay in 1627.

Left: *Queen Henrietta Maria, the French-born wife of King Charles, for whom the province of Maryland was named.* Right: *King Charles I of England, who granted a tract of land in the New World to Lord Baltimore in 1632.*

George Calvert, the first Lord Baltimore

suaded them that he meant no harm. The four soon returned with twenty others from their nearby village. The English watched as the Indians seemed to discuss something. Soon they saw several men, women, and children approach, bringing food, water, and furs. In turn, the English gave gifts to the Nanticokes. Forgetting the hostilities of the previous day, the Nanticokes agreed to serve as guides for Smith as he continued to explore the Kuskarawaok, later to be called the Nanticoke River.

Unfortunately, Smith did not record very much information about the Nanticoke. He did, however, describe them as "the best Marchants of all other Salvages." In Algonquian (the group of languages spoken by most Indians of northeastern North America), the word *Nanticoke* has been translated as "the Tidewater People." Smith noted that there were 200 warriors living with their families in the villages on the Nanticoke River. This meant that the Nanticoke had a larger population than any other tribe on the Eastern Shore.

In 1632 King Charles I of England granted to George Calvert, the first Lord Baltimore, a large tract of land in the New World. The charter described this area as lying north of Virginia and south of New England. The grant specifically included the "land hitherto unsettled" from the Potomac River to a line "which lieth under the fortieth degree north latitude from the quinoctal" and westward from the Atlantic Ocean to a line due north from the "first fountain of the Potomac." The entire province was named Maryland in honor of Charles's wife, Henrietta Maria. Later, the states both of Delaware and Maryland would be formed within these boundaries.

When Lord Baltimore died in 1632, his son Cecil received the charter for the New World land from the king and carried on his father's plan to establish a colony in Maryland. Much-needed settlers were lured by advertisements in London newspapers promising free land and, even more important, freedom of worship. Lord Baltimore planned for his colony to be a safe place for people of his own Catholic faith, but he also invited people of other beliefs to settle there. Leonard Calvert, the new Lord Baltimore's brother, was to be governor. In the spring of 1634, 200 colonists set sail on the *Ark* and the *Dove*. After a long voyage, they came ashore on Blakiston Island in the Potomac River.

The Indians living in what is today southern Maryland gave these colonists a friendly welcome. Maryland authorities recorded that Archihu, chief of the Potomac Indians, told them: "We will eat at the same table; my followers too shall go to hunt for you; and we will have all things in common." The Piscataway and some other tribes in the area readily agreed to sell some of their land, including their villages, to Lord Baltimore. These tribes, fearing the frequent raids of the Susquehannock Indians, who lived further north along the Susquehanna River, had already decided to move their villages inland along the Potomac River.

Living together in peace and harmony would prove to be very difficult for the settlers and the Indians. The colonists hoped to convert the Indians to Christianity. They wanted to trade for furs and possess and cultivate the land. Over the years the Nanticoke, like so many other tribes on the Atlantic seaboard, would meet Europeans whose attitude toward the American Indian ranged from outright hate to brotherly love. Some colonists were treacherous, mistrustful, or indifferent. Others were honorable, concerned, and trustworthy. Some tried to live with the Indians. Some tried to convert them. Only a few would try very hard to understand them. ▲

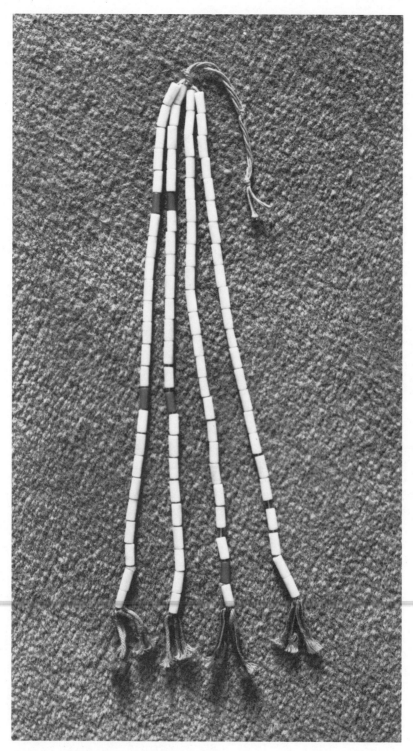

A string of Nanticoke wampum.

DAILY LIFE
OF THE
TIDEWATER PEOPLE

Because Captain Smith and his fellow adventurers recorded very little about the daily life of the Nanticoke, we must depend on other sources for information about them and the other tribes on the Eastern Shore. Archaeological data, brief accounts by other European observers, and information from later historical sources all help us to learn about the way of life, or culture, of these people.

The geography of this area also can help us to understand its people and the world in which they lived. There are three main geographical regions within Maryland; from east to west they are the coastal plain, the piedmont, and the Appalachian Mountains.

The eastern part of what is now Maryland is the coastal plain, divided into two parts by Chesapeake Bay (see map on page 21). These parts are called the Western Shore and the Eastern Shore of Maryland. The state of Delaware also lies within the coastal plain of the Eastern Shore. Five large rivers and many smaller ones empty into the Chesapeake. There are many creeks, swamps, and tide-covered marshes; hence the area is frequently referred to as the tidewater. The coastal plain is low and flat with sandy and light-textured soils. Deer, small animals, and many different species of birds live in the marshes. The waters of the Chesapeake contain a variety of animal life, too—oysters, clams, crabs, and many species of fish.

West of the coastal plain are the low rolling hills of the Piedmont. In some places the hills rise to a height of 880 feet. This area, which has very fertile soils, leads up to the Appalachian Mountains. Great Backbone Mountain in Garrett County rises to a height of 3,360 feet. Deep, beautiful gorges cut by many rivers form natural pathways through the mountains. The mountain slopes are covered with forests which shelter many different types of wildlife.

Over the past several thousand years, the geography of this region has undergone tremendous change. Many different people lived in Maryland during this long period of time. All the people who lived there developed successful ways to survive by using the natural resources of the land. Unfortunately, we cannot know the names of all of these people, because they had no way of writing their languages. The written history of the Maryland and Delaware tidewater people begins with the arrival of Europeans, but by that time, the tidewater people and their ancestors had been in the area for several thousand years.

Instead of reading a written record, archaeologists and other social scientists must study such peoples' lives through the objects they left behind. Artifacts such as arrowheads, spearpoints, axes, pottery, and the places where these people lived give us information that lets us understand their way of life. One of the first things an archaeologist tries to determine is the age of the artifacts. Study of the artifacts left by early Eastern Shore peoples has led archaeologists to divide the prehistory of these cultures into the Paleo-Indian Period, the Archaic Period, and the Woodland Period.

The ancestors of American Indians probably migrated to North America some time between 25,000 and 14,000 years before the present (B.P.). They most likely came from Asia, crossing the Bering Strait into what is now Alaska. This Bering Strait route was probably used, on and off, over a period of several thousand years. Gradually the migrants spread across the continent, reaching the Middle Atlantic area between 13,000 and 10,000 B.P.

In 1927 archaeologists discovered the first real evidence of these early hu-

man inhabitants of North America. An archaeologist named J. D. Figgins dug up the skeleton of a prehistoric bison near the town of Folsom, New Mexico. This bison belonged to the species *Bison taylori*, which became extinct nearly 10,000 years ago. Figgins found a stone weapon (called a projectile point by archaeologists) lying between the bison's ribs. The Folsom point, as it became known, was a slender piece of stone about two inches long. It had been carefully chipped out of a larger piece of stone, and a long narrow flake was removed from each side, leaving sharp edges. Later, many other Folsom points were found at Folsom and several other sites.

Today, we know a great deal about the early hunters who made and used Folsom points. These people are commonly called Paleo-Indians. (*Paleo* means "old" or "ancient".) The Paleo-Indians lived 10,000 and more years

ASIA TO NORTH AMERICA MIGRATION

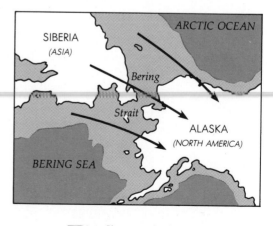

■ Late Pleistocene land bridge
300 feet below present sea level

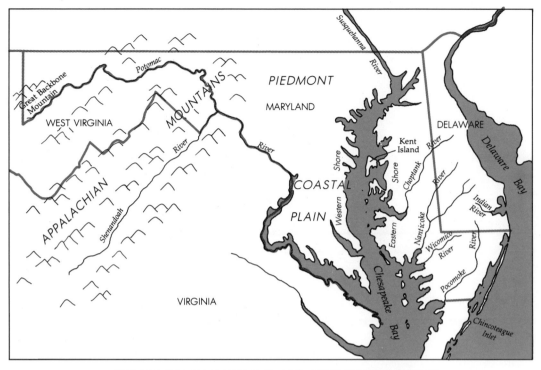

GEOGRAPHY OF MARYLAND AND NEIGHBORING STATES

ago. At that time, known as the Pleistocene Period, the climate of North America was much colder than it is today. Glaciers, sheets of ice, covered much of the northern half of the continent, extending into what is now Pennsylvania and other northern states. These glaciers contained so much water that the level of the sea was lower than it is today. The land area extended further than today's shorelines. This is why there was dry land reaching from Asia to Alaska, where the water of the Bering Strait is today. During the Pleistocene, what is now Chesapeake Bay was also land.

There exists only a scattering of archaeological evidence that Paleo-Indians ever lived in the Maryland and Delaware area. However, more than 100 stone weapon points, many of the Folsom type, have been found lying on the surface of the ground. Although these cannot be precisely dated, they strongly suggest that Paleo-Indians were established in the area. Archaeologists have to use more extensive information from Paleo-Indian sites in neighboring states to help them understand how these early hunters lived. Many animals that are now extinct were able to live in the cold climate of the Pleistocene Period. The mammoth, the great bison, the ground sloth, the saber-toothed tiger, the dire wolf, and other large animals roamed over the vast grasslands beyond the ice sheets. Paleo-Indians depended on these animals for their food and organized into small, seminomadic bands to hunt them. Each band moved from one place to another in its area, hunting the large game animals that provided materials for making clothing and tools as well as food.

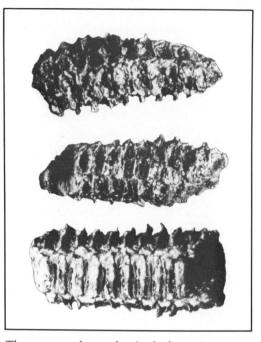

Barbed and notched projectile points, made and used 11,000 years ago.

These corn cobs, carbonized after many centuries in the ground, were found by Delaware archaeologists.

They also depended on other types of food, such as nuts, berries, roots, and small game and fish.

During certain times of the year, the bands would separate, each band moving to a location where it could easily hunt. The Paleo-Indians butchered the animals for meat and skins and mined for stones to make weapon points and other tools. At other times several bands would come together to make a larger base camp. Here members of different families could socialize, exchanging stories and arranging marriages.

About 10,000 years ago the climate of North America began to become warmer and drier. The glaciers gradually melted; their edges retreated northward. As the glaciers melted, the sea level was raised, thus creating Chesapeake Bay and numerous rivers. As the climate warmed, forests began to re-

place the grasslands, and more types of vegetation flourished. The big game animals were unable to adjust to these climatic changes. Over a period of time, the mammoth, the camel, the horse, and other large animals became extinct in North America, because they could not thrive in the new forest environment. Smaller game animals, especially the deer, became an important source of food and clothing for the Indians.

As their environment changed, the early Indians were forced to make great adjustments in their way of life. A new way of life developed as the Pleistocene ended. The Archaic Period, as the time was known, lasted from approximately 10,000 to 3,000 years B.P. As big game hunting became less reliable, the Archaic people depended more on fishing, and gathering wild plant food became more important. Since the Indians did not have to travel as much to locate food, they set up villages where they could stay for longer periods of time.

The new and more abundant plant and animal resources allowed the Archaic people to live in smaller and more defined areas. They lived in bands of perhaps 25 to 50 people. One of the most important changes during the Archaic Period was the invention of improved weapons. Archaic hunters learned how to stalk animals in the forest and strike them down with barbed or notched points. They made chopping and scraping tools of polished stone, using stone axes, for example, to clear away trees for settlement sites and construct log canoes. As the Chesapeake Bay became deeper, the Archaic people learned to harvest oysters, crabs, and other marine foods. They discovered how to prepare certain seeds and nuts by milling them with grinding stones to make them edible. They carved bowls out of solid pieces of soapstone to use for cooking.

The Archaic people lived in pit houses built in the ground. These dwellings were large oval or rectangular pits, cavities dug out of the earth. They had flat floors and walls that were steeply sloped or vertical. The sides were covered with bark supported by poles driven into the earth around the pit floor. There were central hearths for cooking food and heating the dwelling. Archaeologists have found the remains of one pit house in Delaware. It was an irregular oval in shape, about 10.4 feet at its longest point and 9 feet at its wid-

est—the size of a small bedroom. It was 3.6 feet deep.

Because they did not know how to grow their own food and did not keep any domestic animals, the Archaic people had to travel with the change of seasons to find food. They followed the same route year after year, keeping close to their sources of fish and shellfish, meat, berries, and roots, and returning to the same camps and villages season after season.

While the fairly simple Archaic culture was still present in Maryland and Delaware, new developments were taking place further to the south. Indians living in Mexico and further south, in Middle America, were learning to plant certain crops—corn, beans, and squash—and make pottery. The Maya and other higher civilizations of Mexico and South America were culturally more advanced than those occupying what is now the eastern United States. In the southern civilizations, the way of life became extremely complex. People developed elaborate art, rituals, and governments. Villages grew larger, house construction more complicated, tools more specialized. From about 3000 B.P. on, some of these new practices gradually entered North America. The result in the eastern United States was the Woodland Period. Archaeologists have found evidence of the introduction of agriculture, the creation and use of pottery, larger populations, and complex social and religious institutions.

Even before the first contact with Europeans, the Indians in what is now Maryland and Delaware had broad

Culture Approx. Date	Events	Climate and Habitat	Fauna	Technology	Subsistence Activities	Social Organization
Paleo-Indian 25,000–14,000 B.P.* 14,000–10,000 B.P.	Ancestors of Indians arrive in North America, probably crossing the Bering Strait Paleo-Indians reach east coast of North America	Pleistocene—glaciers lower water levels, extend shore lines; grassland habitat	large mammals such as mammoth, great bison, ground sloth, saber-toothed tiger, dire wolf, caribou, horse, camel	worked stone projectile points dating to 14,000 B.P., found in Folsom, New Mexico; Folsom-like points found	hunting large animals; gathering roots, nuts, fruits, berries	small, semi-nomadic hunting bands
Archaic Period 10,000–3,000 B.P.		warming—glaciers melt, water level rises, shores recede; deep bays and rivers form; forests; seasonal variation	large animals die out; smaller game animals, especially deer; fish, shellfish	barbed or notched points; polished stone choppers and scrapers; grinding stones; log canoes	hunting small game animals; fishing, trapping; collecting shellfish; gathering roots, nuts, fruits, berries	small semi-permanent villages, pit houses, 25–50 people in group; seasonal wandering along same route
Woodland Period 3,000 B.P.–contact with Europeans (16th century)	agriculture and pottery-making reach Atlantic coast from south; trade over wide area	seasonal variation	deer, turkey, rabbit, bear, squirrel, and other small animals; fish and shellfish	wide range of tools for agriculture and food preparation; fishing and trapping equipment; pottery and baskets; shell and wood implements; deerskin clothing	hunting deer, bear, and smaller game; fishing and trapping; cultivation of corn, beans, squash; storage of surpluses	complex social and religious institutions; trade relationships over wide area; wigwam becomes family home

Before the present

trading relationships with Indians in the Ohio River area. Objects known to have been created by people of the Adena culture of the Ohio Valley have been found along the Eastern Shore. These artifacts, such as long clay pipes, copper beads, and one-foot-long ceremonial knives, were traded to Maryland and Delaware Indians in exchange for shell beads and fossil shark teeth. These impressive artifacts were buried with some Indians in special graves placed on hills overlooking the surrounding land.

Gradually, contact with Indians in the Ohio Valley came to an end, but trade continued with other Indians in Pennsylvania, Virginia, and New York.

By A.D. 900 the most important items being traded were shell beads, which were used for decoration and barter. The beads were exchanged for skins and furs and stones such as flint and jasper. By this date the Eastern Shore Indians were planting corn and beans. This new source of food produced surpluses, which the Indians dried and stored to use at a later date. In order to protect their stored food supplies from periodic raids by other tribes, many agricultural communities began to surround their villages with log walls. When the first Europeans arrived early in the seventeenth century, the Maryland Indians were still at war with each other.

The Woodland Indians were excellent farmers, hunters, and gatherers. Agriculture provided much of their food. The Indians divided the year according to the five growing seasons:

- ▲ The budding of spring
- ▲ The earing of corn
- ▲ The summer or highest sun
- ▲ The corn gathering or fall of the leaf
- ▲ The winter or "cohonk" (from co'honk, the sound made by geese)

In each season, characteristic plants and animals were available for food. To make the best use of the resources in their environment, the Indians depended heavily on the kinds of foods available at each time of year. (Anthropologists say that they exploited their habitat by practicing a seasonal subsistence strategy.) In the spring and summer, the women and children planted and tended their gardens. The men would hunt and fish to supplement the diet. In the fall, the crops were harvested, and the food was stored in baskets or underground storage pits. During the harsh winter months, individual families would leave the permanent village settlements and separate from the others, going to their family hunting territories. Here they would hunt bear, early in winter, and deer, turkey, rabbit, and squirrel. In the spring, they would return to the villages to plant their gardens.

All members of the tribe had equal rights to use the land. Each family in the village was allowed to use certain parts of the land for its gardens. To clear the forest for planting, the Indians would either build fires around the trunks of the trees or cut a groove around the trunks with a stone ax. This caused the trees to die. The leaves would fall off, letting sunlight reach the ground. The gardens were planted beneath the dead trees. In a few years these trees would fall, or the Indians would burn them down completely. Later, Europeans would refer to such garden clearings as "Indian fields."

Women and children were responsible for taking care of the crops. First the women would prepare the soil with crooked tree limbs or hoes made of stone, shell, or bone. After the soil was loosened, they would plant seeds for maize (corn), beans, squash, pumpkins, sunflowers, and tobacco. The seeds were planted in small mounds or hills three or four feet apart. The seeds of beans or squash were usually placed in the same mound as corn. Beans helped keep the soil fertile, and squash plants covered the ground to help retain moisture.

The younger children were responsible for weeding the gardens and being "live scarecrows." A high sheltered platform was built in the middle of the field. Young boys sat in these shelters and made loud noises to scare the birds away.

Depending on the season, the women and children gathered various edible wild plants, bird eggs, berries, and nuts such as acorns, chestnuts, hickory nuts, and walnuts. This gave them additional food until the gardens were ready to harvest.

Many types of animals and birds lived in the woods and marshes of Maryland and Delaware. In the fields and forests, the Indian men hunted for wild partridges, turkeys, and other birds. They also hunted squirrels, raccoons, opossums, deer, and bear. Along the marshes, rivers, and the bay, they hunted for ducks and geese. They used bows and arrows or spears to kill large animals, and they set traps or snares to catch smaller animals.

Each tribe claimed the right to use large areas of land as its own hunting ground. The family hunting territories were within the tribe's hunting ground. After leaving the villages at the start of the hunting season, Indian families built their hunting lodges near the mouths of streams and rivers. The men usually hunted every day in order to get enough meat to last their families

through winter. The women butchered the animals and prepared the skins.

Indian men had three ways of hunting deer. They might trap large numbers of deer in a small area by building a circle of fires two or three miles in diameter. Gradually, the men would make the circle smaller, frightening the deer toward the center. Then they killed the deer with bows and arrows. Sometimes the men would drive a herd of deer toward a river. Other men were waiting near the shore, ready to shoot the deer as they approached. An Indian man might also cover himself with a deerskin in order to sneak close enough to a deer to shoot it with a bow and arrow.

Chesapeake Bay and its many tributaries were another important source of food. Because so many of the Indian tribes settled on river or bay shores, fishing was a vital part of their lives. Crabs, shrimp, eels, fish, clams, and oysters were caught. The shells were used for bowls, spoons, and decorations. The Indians knew several different ways to catch fish. Sometimes they used a spear or a bow and arrow; at other times, they caught fish in a net.

An ingenious fishing method called for the construction of weirs. Brush and twigs were driven into the bottoms of streams and shallow rivers to create a V-shaped barrier. In the center of the weir was a narrow opening through which the fish would swim. Then the fish would become trapped in small fenced-in sections or large baskets.

The Indians frequently located their homes near bodies of fresh water. The

A wigwam, reconstructed at the Island Field Museum, Delaware. Branches are lashed to the foundation poles, and there is an opening for smoke to vent at the top.

typical home was a wigwam, a dome-shaped structure about 14 feet wide, 10 feet high, and 20 feet long. To make a wigwam framework, a series of branches and saplings were driven into the ground. These posts were bent and bound together at the top with vines or strips of animal hide. This framework was then covered with sheets of tree bark or woven bulrush mats. The mats on the sides of the wigwams could be lifted to allow air to flow through during the warmer months.

The wigwam usually consisted of one large room that was shared by several families. Sometimes the room was separated into smaller sections by hanging mats. The floor of the wigwam was made of earth. Fires were built directly on the earth floor to provide warmth. Although there was a hole in the roof to allow the smoke to escape, the wigwam often got smoky. People slept in

family groups on low benches set along the side walls. The sleeping benches were made of tree limbs covered with mats.

Most Indians lived in villages. Some villages consisted of just a scattered group of wigwams, while others were constructed like forts, with wigwams near each other and surrounded by log walls. In the temporary hunting camps, the women constructed small wigwams, circular huts covered with grass mats.

The Indians made extensive use of deerskins for their clothing. To make garments for wear during warmer weather, the fur was scraped off the deerskin. The skin was then softened and cut to form the apronlike garment that both men and women wore. The aprons were often decorated with beads or fringe. Cold-weather garments consisted of unscraped deerskins and bear-

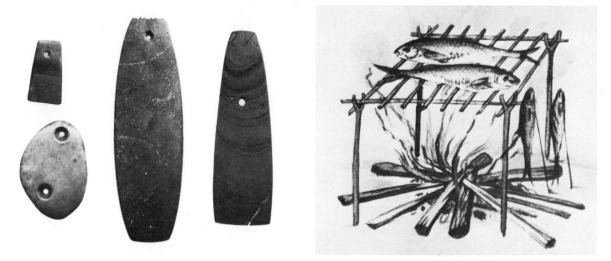

Left: *These stone pendants, which were worn as ornaments, date to* A.D. *740.* Right: *Fish were broiled on a grill of branches, supported by four vertical forked branches inserted into the earth. At right is another method of broiling fish—impaling them on a forked branch, one end of which is inserted into the earth next to a fire.*

skins, with the fur worn on the inside. People wore long cloaks, robes, and leggings. They also had moccasins, made of deerskin or wooden bark. The clothing of the men was usually more elaborately decorated than that of the women.

The Indians wore various ornaments. There were necklaces made from beads, shells, animal bones and teeth, and hand-beaten copper. The copper was obtained by trade from tribes living in the Great Lakes region. The chief of the tribe often wore a special ornament around his neck to mark him as different from the other men. Both men and women wore the same type of hair ornaments, but the men's hairstyles were more elaborate. Other decorations of shell, polished bone, and feathers were attached to clothing. In addition to the ornaments they wore, the Indians sometimes decorated and tattooed their bodies.

Corn was one of the most important Indian foods. Corn could be eaten as a vegetable, made into cornmeal or hominy, or mixed with beans to make succotash. In early summer the young corn was roasted directly in the fire in its green husks and eaten as a vegetable. In late summer the corn was dried and taken off the ears. The kernels were then mixed with lye to remove their hard skins. Then the corn could be ground to make cornmeal or hominy to be eaten in the fall and winter. The dried kernels were placed in mortars, bowl-shaped hollows in a stone or log. The corn was ground into meal with a thick, round stone or stick called a pestle. The cornmeal was mixed with water and baked on flat stones that had been heated in the fire. The result was a kind of bread called *pone*. Instead of butter, Indians ate deer fat with their pone. In early fall the Indians stored a large supply of dried corn and beans in baskets, which were frequently buried in the ground, so they would have food during the winter months when crops did not grow.

Fish was another important food. Fish were broiled by placing them on green wooden racks that stood over a fire. Fish were also impaled on sharpened sticks which were stuck into the ground near the flame.

Indian women made clay pottery for holding water and cooking. One way of making pottery was to roll clay into long ropelike pieces with the palms of their hands. Then they wound the clay ropes into a spiral and coiled one on top of the other to make jars, pots, and bowls of different sizes and shapes. The women carefully pinched and smoothed the clay to join the different layers. Often they decorated the jars by scratching designs into the clay before it hardened, using a sharpened stone or stick. They pressed cloth, nets, or rope onto the wet clay to make other designs. These pots usually had conical bottoms so they could be supported by small stones on a hearth or stand upright in the earth floor of a wigwam.

A wide variety of plants was used to make baskets for carrying and storage. The plant most frequently used was silk grass; others were bulrush, cornhusks, native hemp, bark, and pinecones. Few historical documents mention the weaving methods used to make the baskets. The most common technique appears to have been a simple over-one, under-one weave. A coil technique, however, was used with cornhusks, and a unique method produced decorative strong containers from pinecones and leather.

To make cornhusk baskets, the husks were soaked in water and then twisted until they looked like short

Left: *Vegetables and stews were cooked in a clay pot whose pointed bottom was supported by the bed of wood of the fire. Stones heated in the fire were placed in the pot with the food and quickly heated the contents.* Right: *A net-decorated clay pot of about A.D. 1200, reconstructed from fragments found at an archaeological site in Delaware.*

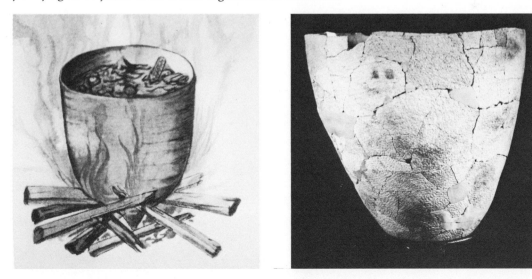

lengths of rope. These were coiled together and sewed with silk grass to hold the basket shape. To make pinecone containers, blades from cones of the yellow pine were sewn, one by one, onto a flat piece of stiff leather. Five of these decorated leather slabs were then laced together with strips of hide to form an open, basketlike container.

The Indians made tools, weapons, and utensils from other materials they found in their environment. Stone, clay, shell, bone, wood, animal hides, and parts of plants were used to make various items. Needles for sewing, for example, were made of polished bone. Strips of animal hide were used as thread and cord. Sharpened flint points were used as awls to pierce holes in hides for sewing and lacing.

Stone tools were used for grinding or pounding. These hammerstones were simple to make because rocks of just the right size and shape were easily found. It usually required more work

and skill to make spearheads, arrowheads, axes, drills, and scrapers. Making these tools involved grinding, chipping, and polishing. A piece of deer antler, which anthropologists call a flaker, was used to shape sharp edges for tools and weapons. The Indians pressed the flaker against the edge of a stone, chipping away one tiny piece after another until the edge became thin. Then they rubbed the edge with a harder stone to sharpen and polish it.

Indian hunters and warriors used bows and arrows, spears, and tomahawks as weapons. The bows were about five feet long. The wooden part of the bow was carved from a branch of an ash, hickory, or locust tree. The bowstring was made from a strip of deerskin or deer sinew.

Arrows were made from light wooden shafts or reeds. A sharp point of bone, horn, or stone was attached at one end. A few feathers at the other end helped to guide the arrow in flight.

Left: *A Nanticoke "fancy basket" made of cornhusks.* Right: *A basketlike container made by fastening individual pine cone blades to leather panels.*

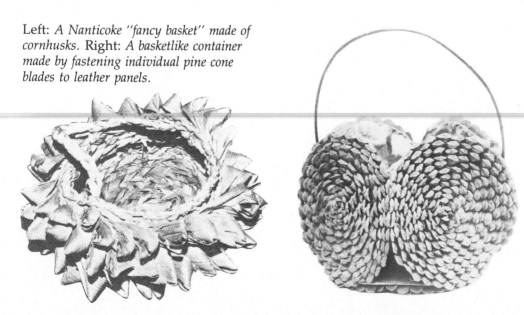

A stone pestle, A.D. 740.

Most warriors and hunters were quite accurate with the bow and arrow.

Spears were like long, heavy arrows. They had large points that could also be used as knives. The earliest tomahawks were simply wooden clubs. Later, a ground and polished stone with a groove around it was attached to the wooden club. This combination tool was used as an ax. A green piece of hickory was bent around the groove and was secured with a strip of damp leather. As the hickory and leather dried they tightened, firmly securing the ax blade in place. After contact with the Europeans, the Indians traded with the colonists to obtain metal tomahawks and axes.

The Indians of the Eastern Shore had a well-developed system of government. In some cases, four to six tribes would organize into a confederacy under one leader, who was called a *tayac*. This person was responsible for making many important decisions for the tribes. In addition to the tayac, each tribe had a major chief, or *werowance*. The werowance gave advice to the tayac and could make some decisions for his own tribe. There were two councils, the peace council, or *wiso*, and the war council, or *cockarouse*. Members of both councils would meet regularly with the werowance. At these meetings, called *matchacomicos*, problems that were important to the tribe were discussed. Tobacco was smoked in ceramic pipes in a formal ceremony or as an offering to the various spirits of the Indian world.

Indians in Maryland and Delaware believed in a variety of spirits. They felt that many things in nature—such as water, lightning, fire, stone, and animals—possessed a unique spirit. To ensure good luck, the Indians would offer sacrifices to the appropriate spirits. They made many sacrifices to Manito, a particularly important spirit who was considered to be the giver of all good things. To Manito the Indians sacrificed the first food of the harvest and the first game of their hunting and fishing. They also made sacrifice to Okee, a powerful evil spirit.

The Indians held religious ceremonies or rituals at several times throughout the year. Ceremonies and rituals were often held in a wigwam that was used only for such purposes and involved special songs, dances, and prayers. Tobacco was smoked in special pipes as a focal point of most religious ceremonies, because the Indians believed smoking tobacco purified them.

Indians in Maryland and Delaware believed they would have another life

The Nanticoke dead were laid for burial in a quiackeson house, similar to the wigwam in construction. This painting by John White shows the side wall mats of the structure lifted to display the interior.

after death. They felt that if they had lived a good life, they would go to a place of great happiness after they died. If they had lived an evil life, however, their afterlife would be one of great pain and suffering.

Many of the Eastern Shore tribes, including the Nanticoke, buried their dead in three stages. After a person died, the body was placed for a brief time in a special structure called a *quiackeson*. In some cases, the bodies were mummified and then placed in the quiackesons. In other cases, after some time, a priest scraped the remaining flesh from the bones and returned them to the quiackeson. The next resting place of the dead was a pit dug in the earth for the bones or mummified bodies. About every five to seven years, all of the bones of the dead would be gathered from the burial pits and buried again in a common grave or ossuary.

The Indians traded or bartered to acquire the things they wanted from other tribes. There were problems with this system, because bartering meant exchanging items of unequal value. Although bartering sometimes worked successfully, the Indians developed a type of money or medium of exchange.

Their medium of exchange was wampum. The Algonquian word *wampumpeaq* means "white strings." Wampum consisted of pieces of clam and oyster shells cut and shaped into beads. There were two types of wampum: peak and roanoke. Peak was made from shell beads that were carefully formed and highly smoothed and polished. Roanoke consisted of broken pieces of unpolished shells that had been drilled with holes and strung on strips of dried animal skin. Peak was two or three times more valuable than roanoke. Wampum was purple or white. The purple wampum was made from the colored part of the clam shell. Because more of the shell was white than colored, there was more white wampum, and it was less valuable than the purple variety.

Wampum was strung on strips of animal hide to form strings or woven into broad belts. The woven wampum had meanings, which the Indians said they "talked" into it, and served as a record of laws, ceremonies, and important events. Strings of wampum were used for bartering and could also serve as messages. No treaty or agreement would be honored unless there had been an exchange of wampum.

Indians in Maryland and Delaware traveled widely to trade with other tribes. The numerous rivers and streams that entered into the Chesapeake Bay were a major means of transportation. Bark canoes and log dugouts glided through these waters, carrying furs and other goods from one Indian village to another.

The Indians also traveled along many trails. The major trails ran through the eastern forests in a north-south direction. But there were east-west routes, too, bringing trade goods from as far away as the Ohio Valley to the tribes in Maryland and Delaware. Noiselessly, moccasined feet journeyed from inland hunting territories to walled villages near the shore. These well-worn trails also served as important trade routes and war paths for the Iroquois tribes, whose people frequently traveled from New York and Canada as far south as the Carolinas.

The Indians' occasional contacts with Europeans in the late 16th and early 17th centuries signaled the end of their familiar way of life. The tranquillity and traditions of the Nanticoke were soon to be challenged by newcomers. The experiences the Nanticoke would have with the white colonists would change their lives forever. ▲

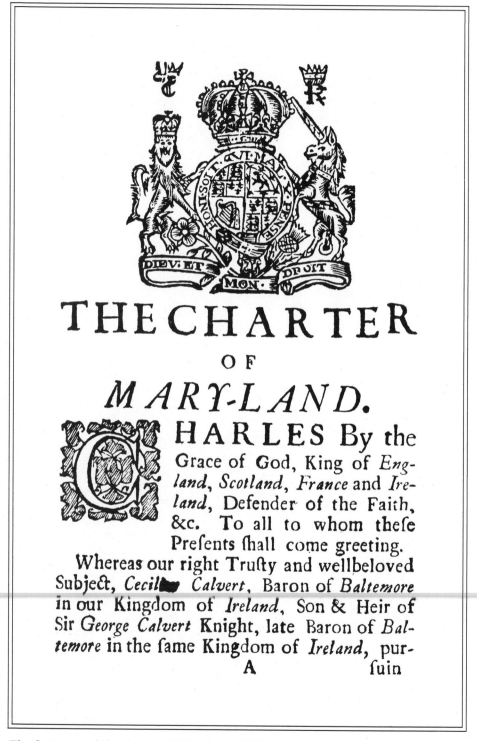

THE CHARTER

OF

MARY-LAND.

CHARLES By the Grace of God, King of *England, Scotland, France* and *Ireland*, Defender of the Faith, &c. To all to whom thefe Prefents fhall come greeting. Whereas our right Trufty and wellbeloved Subject, *Cecil*** *Calvert*, Baron of *Baltemore* in our Kingdom of *Ireland*, Son & Heir of Sir *George Calvert* Knight, late Baron of *Baltemore* in the fame Kingdom of *Ireland*, pur-
fuin

A

The first page of the charter of Maryland, 1632.

THE
NANTICOKE
AND THE
COLONISTS

By the end of the 17th century only the Nanticoke and Choptank Indians were still living on the Eastern Shore of Maryland. They had survived nearly 70 years of mounting pressure and increasing conflict created by continuous contact with white settlers. Many smaller, lesser-known tribes had been forced to leave their villages, joining other tribes in neighboring colonies. Some tribes simply vanished, leaving no evidence of their fate. The Susquehannock Indians resorted to hostility and war to resist the settlers, but they were vanquished. The Piscataway had allied themselves with the colonists for protection, but the Maryland colony later broke this agreement. Many of the Nanticokes ultimately abandoned their villages on the Eastern Shore and migrated to Pennsylvania, New York, and Canada.

In their rush to establish colonies, the English often overlooked or ignored the land rights of the Indians, who lived in most of the territory covered by the original royal grants to private compa-nies and colonists in the New World. The crown granted title to the land, but it left to the discretion of the grantees how to deal with the Indians. Significantly, the Indians were not completely excluded in the Charter of 1632, by which King Charles I granted Maryland to Cecil Calvert, Lord Baltimore. The charter did not specify the rights of the Indians or indicate any concern for their welfare or proper treatment. It did, however, contain four passages that refer to the Indians.

First, the charter recognized that the granted territory was already occupied by Indians. Second, the charter mentioned a payment from the Indians to the settlers requiring "two Indian arrows of those parts to be delivered at the said castle of Windsor." Third, "savages" were cited as potential enemies of the colonists. Finally, the twelfth section of the charter authorized Lord Baltimore to collect troops and wage war on the "barbarians" and other enemies who might threaten the settlements, "to pursue them beyond

The first English settlement in Maryland, St. Mary's City, is shown in this painting based on archaeological findings. The Indian village is just outside the town walls in the lower left. A fortlike wall surrounds the settlement, and there are semicircular bastions at each corner. Many of the settlers' homes are similar in construction to those of the Indians.

the limits of their province," and "if God shall grant it, to vanquish and captivate them; and the captives to put to death, or according to their descretion, to save."

With this charter, the king transferred to Lord Baltimore absolute authority to deal with the Indians' title to, and possession of, the land. Lord Baltimore appointed his brother, Leonard Calvert, governor, and instructed him that upon his arrival in Maryland he was first to choose as a settlement a place that would be "healthful and fruitful," could be easily fortified, and would be convenient for trade both with the English and the Indians.

As the Maryland colonists developed missionary activities among the Indians, established trade with them, and obtained land from them during the 17th century, an Indian policy would gradually take shape. Because the Nanticoke, on the Eastern Shore of Chesapeake Bay, were 50 miles from the seat of the Maryland government at St. Mary's, on the lower Western Shore, the tribe was not among those with whom Governor Calvert dealt at first.

Firsthand dealings with fur traders and colonial settlers, however, did involve the Nanticoke with the growing Maryland colony. The colonial authorities tried at an early date to protect the

(continued on page 41)

THE JOHN WHITE PAINTINGS

John White, whose magnificent watercolors are the earliest authentic pictorial record of life in North America, was the first artist to draw the people, animals, and plants of the New World. White originally came to North America on Martin Frobisher's voyage to Baffin Island in 1577, producing the earliest pictures of Eskimos to be seen in Europe. He next crossed the Atlantic as artist in Sir Walter Raleigh's 1585 expedition and remained a year in the first colony in Virginia, on Roanoke Island in what is now North Carolina. White made a third journey to the American coast in 1587, this time appointed by Raleigh to be governor of a new colony of about 115 men, women, and children. He arrived in Roanoke in July and stayed for one month, during which his daughter gave birth to the first child of European descent to be born in the New World. At the request of his people, White went back to England for supplies and support. When he returned to Virginia in 1590 the Roanoke settlers had disappeared, never to be found. Little is known of White after that last voyage to North America. Most of John White's watercolors of American Indians of the middle Atlantic coast were done during his 1585 trip to Roanoke. These paintings later illustrated the 1588 book **Briefe and True Report of the New Found Land of Virginia**, which was written by his fellow traveler, scientist Thomas Heriot, and intended to stimulate interest in the new colony.

White painted the wife of a chief of Secoton. She wears a deerskin apron as well as a necklace and a headband of beads. Her face, arms, and legs are decorated with body painting.

The Indians caught fish in nets held at the end of long poles, which were also used to propel a canoe noiselessly through the water. At left is a weir or gatelike fish trap made of branches stretched across the river. Spear fishing is shown at rear. For light at night, the Indians kept a fire going in the center of the canoe. Its blaze may have blinded the fish so they could not see the nets or weir.

An Indian man wearing winter dress, a fringed deerskin robe with the fur inside and moccasins. Men's hair was cut short on both sides, leaving a crest running down the center of the head from the forehead to the nape of the neck. Animal grease kept the hair shining and stiff.

The village of Secoton on the Pamlico River. The fields at the right show three stages in growing corn, with full-grown corn at the top. In the lower right are dancers in a circle marked with carved posts, with several dancers crouching as they wait their turn to join the circle.

The Indian village of Pomeiooc. White paid particular attention to the construction of houses, which were made of a wood frame covered with woven mats or sheets of tree bark. White shows the interiors of some of the dwellings so that the raised sleeping platforms can be seen. The palisade of "small poles thick together" was for protection against enemies.

A council of Indians meets around a campfire.

(continued from page 36)

Indians' "privileges" of hunting, fishing, and crabbing, but their warnings to settlers went unheeded. The Indians' traditional hunting and farming activities were disrupted almost immediately, and the Nanticoke and other tribes apparently tried to supplement their diet by stealing and killing the domestic hogs and cattle of the settlers. The colonists complained of this on numerous occasions.

In 1666 an Eastern Shore Indian named Mattagund presented the Indians' view of these conflicts. He appealed to Maryland officials to "Let us have no Quarrels for killing Hogs no more than for the Cows Eating the Indian corn. Your hogs & Cattle injure Us You come too near Us to live & Drive Us from place to place. We can fly no farther let us know where to live & how to be secured for the future from the Hogs & Cattle."

The Nanticoke had to cope with an increasing number of settlers and the unfair and at times illegal practices of traders. Between 1642 and 1698 they attempted to protect themselves and their land by frequently staging raids or threatening war. In 1642 and again in 1647, Captain John Price, a member of the Governor's Council and commander of a permanent militia, sailed with about 40 armed men across Chesapeake Bay to put an end to these attacks.

Price had been ordered by Thomas Greene, then governor of Maryland, to show no mercy to the Nanticoke. He was to destroy their corn, burn their houses, and kill them or take them prisoners. The goal of these harsh measures was to prevent the Nanticoke from planting corn, hunting, or fishing, in order to make them poor and famished and too weak to take hostile action against the colony. Captain Price attacked the villages of the Nanticoke and the nearby Wiccomiss, but he did not succeed in completely vanquishing them. Settlers on the Eastern Shore continued for several years to complain about raids by the Nanticoke and other tribes in the area.

A threat from the well-organized Susquehannock Indians kept the colony's military forces occupied, so the governor could not raise another force to send against the tribes on the Eastern Shore. The Susquehannock, however, were being relentlessly attacked from the north by the Iroquois, who sought to extend their territory further south. In desperation, the Susquehannock turned to the colonists for help. In exchange for their friendship and military alliance, the Maryland authorities demanded that the Susquehannock relinquish their claim to jurisdiction over the Eastern Shore as far south as the Choptank River. On July 5, 1652, the Susquehannock Indians signed a treaty with Maryland. Tradition has it that the signing took place under the poplar tree that still stands in front of St. John's College in Annapolis. (It is known as "the Liberty Tree" because during the American Revolution local patriots gathered around it to discuss political events.)

Soon after the treaty with the Susquehannock, the governor of Maryland received a petition from the inhabitants of Kent Island, in Chesapeake Bay, just across from Annapolis. The settlers reported that the Indians had killed two settlers and wounded another. They asked the governor to "take Some Speedy Course for the Suppressing of these Heathens, and avenging of Guiltless Blood, and the preservation of our lives with our Wives and Children." With no fear of reprisals from the Susquehannock, Maryland could now take full-scale military action against all of the Eastern Shore tribes. An armed force prepared to take action, but its captain advised the governor to postpone the operation because of severe weather and the Indians' foreknowledge of the campaign. The expedition apparently never took place.

By 1668, however, the Nanticoke were under the complete control of the Maryland authorities. On May 1, 1668, the tayac Unnacokasimmon signed the first of five separate treaties attempting to secure peaceful relations between the province of Maryland and the Nanticoke. This first treaty sought to establish "an Inviolable peace & Amity between the Right Honorable the Lord Proprietor of this province, and the Emperor of the Nanticoke to the World's End to Endure," and agreed that "all former Acts of Hostility & Damages whatsoever by either Party susteyned to be buried in perpetual Oblivion." "Emperor" was the title used by the English for the chief or tayac.

The Nanticoke no longer posed a significant threat to the colony. For this reason, they were at a weak point in negotiating the treaties, and the resulting documents were one-sided and did not recognize the Nanticoke's demands. They were required by these treaties, for instance, to lay down their weapons and hold up their hands tied with white cloth when they approached an English settler's plantation and to hand over to Maryland officials for punishment any individuals who murdered or plundered a settler.

Despite the peace treaties, friction continued between the Nanticoke and the colonists. In 1677 and 1678 the Nanticoke raided plantations on both the Western and Eastern Shores of Maryland. Not until 1682 were soldiers sent to punish the offenders. In 1687 rumors circulated among the English that the Nanticoke were planning an uprising against the colony.

Throughout this period, the settlers continued to take and occupy illegally the land of the Nanticoke and other tidewater tribes. Completely frustrated by the loss of their land, the Nanticoke and the nearby Choptank requested that the authorities issue a grant legally giving them certain tracts of land. The Maryland assembly responded by establishing three reservations in the late 17th and early 18th centuries.

The first reservation in Maryland was created for the Choptank Indians in 1669. In 1698 the assembly passed an act to create a reservation for the Nanticoke Indians of Dorchester County, but the legislation was repealed because of a dispute over the reservation boundaries. In 1704 an identical act was passed to define the boundaries of the Chiconi Reservation, named for Chickawan Creek. In 1711 the Maryland assembly provided an additional 3,000 acres of land for the Nanticoke on Broad Creek. Later, all of the reservation land would be highly desirable to the new Americans of Maryland, but at the time the reservations were set up, the shore areas along the rivers and creeks had attracted few settlers. It was a marginal environment, considered unsuitable for agriculture.

The creation of reservations did prevent some further encroachment on the Indians' land by the settlers, but it also led to two critical new problems. First, the Nanticoke's seasonal food-gathering activities were disrupted. Because the Nanticoke needed to travel between their traditional hunting and farming sites, they would not be able to secure enough food if they were restricted to the reservations. The second problem was a misunderstanding of the words in the legislation, "so long as they shall occupy and live upon the same." The clause required the Nanticoke to occupy the reservations throughout the year. If they failed to do so, the law stated that the land would be taken back by the governor of Maryland.

In 1711, less than a decade after the Nanticoke moved to the Chiconi Reservation, they bitterly complained that the land there was worn out and insufficient for their use. They requested

A Maryland plantation in the 18th century. Plantation owners depended on slave labor to raise and harvest their major crops, corn and tobacco.

additional land, and Maryland granted them 3,000 acres on Broad Creek. The Nanticoke continued to be plagued by the "repeated and excessive trespass" on their land by white settlers. Once again the Maryland assembly sought to prevent these offenses. The assembly assured the Nanticoke of their "free and uninterrupted possession of the tract lying between the North Fork of the Nanticoke River and Chicucone [Chiconi] Creek . . . so long as they or any of them should think fit to use and not totally desert and quit the same." To

IMPORTANT LOCATIONS IN NANTICOKE HISTORY

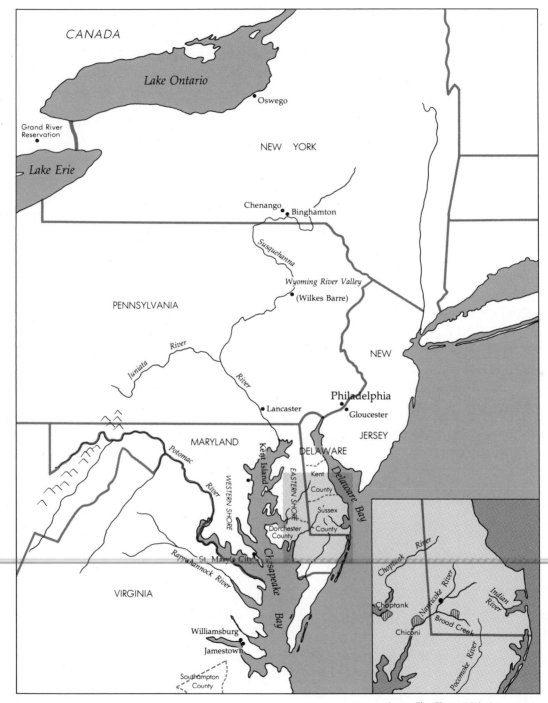

Inset: The Three 18th-Century
Maryland Reservations

further prevent settlers from gaining this property, the Nanticoke were not allowed to sell or lease their land to the settlers.

Despite these protective measures, the abuse and disregard of the Nanticoke's right to occupy the reservations continued. Some trespassers destroyed Indian land by cutting large amounts of timber and then refused to pay the Indians for any damages. In complete violation of the laws, some people rented directly from the Indians and settled on Indian land and then failed to pay the agreed-upon rent. Some secretly purchased the land from the Indians and built their homesteads, but others simply were squatters (people who settled on land without a legal title) on the land and assumed ownership by right of occupancy.

Although the Nanticoke tried to reside within the boundaries of their reservations, they were repeatedly hampered by the colonists' continual encroachment on their land. When they went into the woods to hunt and build temporary shelters, the Indians recounted, "some of the White people when we go out of them will set them on fire and burn them down to the ground and leave us Destitute of any Cover to Shelter us from the weather."

One incident vividly shows the conflict between the Indians on reservations and the settlers who desired to gain possession of their land. In 1723 Captain John Rider and Isaac Nicholls, two Maryland settlers, claimed that they had legal possession of a large tract of land on an Indian reservation because they had found the reservation deserted except for one Indian. The lone Indian was William Ashquash, son of the late Nanticoke tayac. Testimony in court established that Rider had physically ousted Ashquash and set his cabin on fire. Rider had then built a clapboard house for himself on that land. The Nanticoke, returning in the fall, resumed living on their land and burned down Rider's house. They testified that Rider had indeed found their towns uninhabited, but not because they had abandoned their land. They were merely following their traditional routes, making their seasonal migrations to their customary food sources. They had "gone out to their hunting quarters according to their usual practice." The Maryland authorities ruled that Rider and Nicholls were trespassing and had no right or title to the land. Settlers continually tried to justify such actions by claiming that the Indian land appeared to be deserted and abandoned.

In 1759 a delegation of Indians from the Eastern Shore took their complaints directly to Governor Horatio Sharpe. The Indians told the governor that they were few in number, suffered from a shortage of food, and were being violently forced off their land. They appealed to him to consider their "Pitiful Scituation and Condition if we cannot have the freedom and Privilege which we were allowed of in Antient Times."

Still another problem was a by-product of increased trade. By now many

Governor Horatio Sharpe of Maryland, to whom the Nanticoke complained in 1759 about the abuse of their rights by the colonists.

settlers were traveling through the area, trading various goods for furs and skins. While visiting the Nanticoke reservations, some unscrupulous traders would bring quantities of alcoholic beverages to trade for furs. Like all Indians, the Nanticoke had never tasted alcoholic beverages before the arrival of the Europeans. They could not realize the ill effects of liquor and easily fell victim to the pleasant sensations caused by rum and whiskey. After a drunken Indian woke up, he often discovered that he had traded all of his valuable furs for liquor instead of for tools, clothing, or other goods.

The Nanticoke leaders tried on several occasions to have the Maryland authorities punish any trader who brought liquor into their villages. Such laws were passed by the Maryland assembly, but it was almost impossible to enforce them in the distant parts of the colony.

European politics were also being imported to the New World. France, at war with England in the Old World, tried to unite various tribes in Maryland and Pennsylvania to revolt against the English. In 1742, disgusted after a century of abuse, hostility, and misunderstanding, the Nanticoke decided to make a last stand. They agreed to join this uprising. The Eastern Shore Indians met in Winnasoccum swamp, along the Pocomoke River, to join in a war dance.

Fortunately for the Maryland colonists, a Choptank Indian, friendly with the settlers, informed the authorities. The plot came to an abrupt end. The Maryland assembly severely reprimanded the Nanticoke for their part in the conspiracy. The authorities informed the Nanticoke that the colony had the power to take all the tribe's land and punish the tribe's members for their part in the revolt. But, they added, "we are rather desirous to use you kindly like Brethren in hopes that it will beget the same kindness in You to Us."

The Nanticoke were unmoved by this offer of friendship. When the plot failed, they realized that their relationship with the Maryland colonists would never improve, nor would it let them

INDIAN PLACE NAMES

Many place names used by Indians have remained in use.
Here are some Algonquian words, and their meanings in English,
describing places and geographical features. Most of them
are identified on the maps on pages 21 and 44.

ALLEGHENY *beautiful stream*

CATOCTIN *speckled mountain*

CHESAPEAKE *great shellfish bay*

CHICONE *big snow*

CHINCOTEAGUE *it is lifted up* or *set up high*

CHOPTANK *it flows in the opposite direction*

MATTAPONI *meeting of waters*

POCOMOKE *it is pierced* or *broken ground*

POTOMAC *where goods are brought in*

SUSQUEHANNA *smooth flowing stream*

WICOMICO *pleasant dwelling* or *village*

live in their traditional way and in peace. Two years later, they sent a delegation to the Maryland authorities. Maryland had passed legislation requiring any Indian to apply for permission before leaving the colony. They requested permission to leave the province and live among the Six Nations of the Iroquois, a powerful confederation of tribes that lived in New York, Pennsylvania, and Canada.

The Iroquois had an ulterior motive for inviting the Nanticoke and other tribes to join them. They wanted help in asserting their claim to land, in order to keep European settlers from taking additional territory. In return, the Iroquois offered protection to the smaller tribes who joined them.

The Nanticoke did not all leave the Eastern Shore of Maryland at one time. Beginning in 1744, individual families left their villages and paddled their canoes up the Susquehanna River into Pennsylvania. Near Lancaster, Pennsylvania, the Reverend Christian Pyrlaeus wrote in his memorandum book on May 21, 1748, that he had seen several of the Nanticoke from Maryland pass by in 10 canoes on their way to the Wyoming Valley of Pennsylvania. This move to Pennsylvania was to be permanent.

The Reverend John Heckewelder, a missionary who had spent many years among the Lenni Lenape Indians in southeastern Pennsylvania, recalled that the Nanticoke in Pennsylvania returned to the Eastern Shore on several occasions. They went to their old homes to fetch the bones of their dead so that the deceased members of the tribe could be reburied near the new villages.

By 1748 a majority of the Nanticoke had moved into Pennsylvania, settling first near the Juniata River. Another group had established a village at Chenango, near present-day Binghamton in New York. Soon after constructing the village at Juniata, delegates from the Nanticoke and several other tribes complained to the governor and council of Pennsylvania that settlers were encroaching on their land along the Juniata River. Within a short time the Nanticoke moved to the Wyoming Valley, only to be forced out in 1755 because of the outbreak of hostilities between the French and English settlers. By 1765 the Nanticoke had temporarily resided at Oswego, Chugnut,

and Chenango in upstate New York. From New York, the Nanticoke émigrés next went into Canada, where they came completely under the control of the Six Nations.

The number of Nanticoke living on the Grand River Reservation in Ontario, Canada, during the late 18th and early 19th century was small when compared to the population of the Iroquois. The tribe played only a minor role in the political affairs and economy of the reservation. The following figures reflect the small number of Nanticoke living on the Grand River Reservation at that time:

1785	11
1810	9
1811	10
1813	2
1843	47

Nearly two decades after many Nanticokes began to leave the Eastern Shore, there was still a remnant of the tribe in their homeland in Maryland. Those who remained on the Eastern Shore started proceedings to sell what land they still had in Maryland. Sir William Johnson, superintendent of Indian affairs for England's northern colonies, wrote to Governor Horatio Sharpe in 1767, asking him to give the Nanticoke assistance and protection in the selling of their land. The following year the assembly passed "An Act for Granting to the Nanticoke Indians a compensation for the lands therein mentioned." The Nanticoke received $666.66 in ex-

In 1752 Baltimore was a village of only 25 houses. Fishing and agriculture were the occupations of all settlers in this typical colonial town.

change for relinquishing their claim to any land in the province of Maryland.

Meanwhile, a small remnant of Choptank Indians continued to live on their reservation. Later observers would often confuse the Choptank with the Nanticoke. The Choptank had hoped to preserve its people and customs by staying on the reservation, but its population dwindled. In 1798 the Maryland assembly appointed commissioners to purchase the land still belonging to the Choptanks. A tract not to exceed 100 acres was to be set aside for their use. It was to include their settlements and a sufficient amount of nearby woodlands. Only three years later, after Molley Mulberry, the last member of the tribe, died and left no heirs, the legislators assumed control of the remaining Choptank land.

One of the most significant consequences of contact between the Nanticoke and European settlers was the tremendous decline in the Indian population. In the early 17th century, according to Captain John Smith, the Nanticoke numbered between 2,000 and 3,000 persons. In 1756 it was estimated that only about 140 Indians were still in Maryland, living on the reservations. By the end of the 18th century, it was generally agreed that no Indians remained in Maryland, but in reality, several Nanticoke families were still living on the Eastern Shore. ▲

Wooden mortars used for grinding corn.

ADJUSTMENTS
AND
TRIALS

The Nanticokes who chose to remain on the Eastern Shore in the 18th century were able to survive because of their family hunting territory system. The family hunting group might consist of a single nuclear family—parents and children—or of a few related nuclear families. All family members had the right to hunt, trap, and fish in the family's inherited district. The family hunting territory was bounded by specific rivers, lakes, or other natural landmarks and was often known by certain local names identified with the family itself. This long-established practice of small hunting groups dispersing in the woods resulted in families being isolated from other families in the tribe. Many families lived for long periods at a time in their own territories.

Success in hunting in the family territory required a sizable and stable local population of animals. The number of suitable hunting territories in the Nanticoke's area was limited by the supply of animals. The ecological balance of the animal population required that the number of animals killed be replaced by the birth of new animals every year. The arrival of English settlers upset this long-established ecological balance in the Nanticoke River area. The settlers hunted, too, depleting the animal population below the natural replacement level. They also cleared forestland for their plantations, destroying the animals' natural food sources, which resulted in even fewer animals living within a narrower range. This seriously jeopardized the food resources of several of the family hunting groups along the Nanticoke River. Some Nanticokes could depend on hospitality and aid from those families whose territories were untouched. Gradually, though, the settlers' destruction of the environment spread. All the major plant and animal food sources in the area were affected. Those families whose hunting territories were most damaged were among the first to leave for Pennsylvania, New York, and Canada.

Even more wanted to leave. Representatives of the Six Nations of the

Iroquois, speaking on behalf of their Nanticoke "Couzins," told Pennsylvania officials in 1749 that Maryland was refusing to give the remaining Nanticoke permission to leave. "You know that on some differences between the People of Maryland & them we went for them & placed them at the Mouth of Juniata, where they now live; they came to Us while on our Journey & told us that there were [three] Settlements of their Tribe left in Maryland . . . ," the Iroquois stated, probably referring to the three Maryland reservations.

Pennsylvania officials continued to hear about the problems of the tribes remaining in Maryland. In 1761 some Nanticoke and the Piscataway people formally requested permission to leave for those who were still living in the province of Maryland. "About seven years ago we went down to Maryland with a Belt of Wampum to fetch our Flesh and Blood . . . [but] they would

not let our Flesh and Blood then come away with us," they would later complain. In response, the governor of Pennsylvania stated: "As I am not Governor of that province, I have no Power to order the People there to suffer their Relations to come away from them." The Nanticoke complained again to Pennsylvania authorities about this situation in 1776.

There were indeed several Nanticoke families remaining on the Eastern Shore of Maryland after 1745. Not all wanted to leave, and most may have been quite comfortable in their familiar surroundings. They, and related Indians throughout the region, apparently depended on their family hunting system in or near their traditional territories. At first, the remaining family hunting groups chose to live in places that were isolated from the villages and farmsteads of the colonists. Swamps, islands, or out-of-the-way necks of land

The Nanticoke River in Maryland, shown here in a 1922 photograph by anthropologist Frank Speck, probably looked much as it did 200 years earlier.

were favorite locations. After years of conflict, the Nanticoke wanted as little contact as possible with the outside world. They moved into sites that were unattractive to the Europeans. These areas were not fit for large plantations and commercial agriculture. They did not have good transportation connections to ports on navigable rivers or along the Chesapeake Bay. However, these locations did provide adequate food resources to meet the basic needs of a small number of Nanticoke family groups.

Eighteenth-century descriptions depict these Eastern Shore environments as bleak and unforgiving. Until 1759, wrote the author of a "Description of the Cypress Swamps in Delaware and Maryland States," the land in this area was considered to be of little value. Lewis Evans, an explorer and mapmaker, described the shores of Delaware Bay as "low, flat Marshes, void of Trees & lie mostly unimproved." The few Europeans who did settle in the area were widely separated from each other.

Throughout the 18th century, there were references by early settlers to Indians living in these isolated areas of Maryland, Virginia, and Sussex County, Delaware. One such report came from the Reverend George Ross, who had been directed by the Methodist church to preach to the Indians. Ross complained that he could hardly find any Indians to preach to. "The Indians have their abodes a great way back in the Woods, so that we seldom see or converse with one another, unless it be when leaving their Winter Quarters they straggle up and down among the English plantations and villages to meet with Chapman for their burthen of Skins, or with a meal of Victuals."

Another description of Indians in this area came from John Fontaine, who had a large plantation in King William County, Virginia. In 1715, while traveling from Williamsburg to the German colony on the Rappahannock River, he encountered a remnant of the once powerful Indians of Virginia:

> We see by the side of the road an Indian cabin built with posts put into the ground, the one by the other as close as they could stand, and about seven feet high, all of an equal length. It was built four-square, and a sort of roof upon it, covered with bark of trees. They say it keeps out the rain very well. The Indian women were all naked, only a girdle they had tied around the waist, and about a yard of blanketing put between their legs, and fastened one end under the fore-part of the girdle, and the other behind. Their beds were mats of bulrushes, upon which they lie, and have one good blanket to cover them. All the household goods was a pot.

The Reverend David Humphreys, another Methodist preacher, observed in 1730 that the number of Indians (in all probability the Nanticoke) in Sussex County, Delaware, did not exceed 120. They had a small settlement on the distant border of his parish where it bordered Maryland. He described them as "extremely barbarous and obstinately ignorant."

In 1759 Andrew Burnaby, who traveled throughout Virginia, observed a group of Pamunkey Indians. His description shows how the life of the Pamunkey and other similarly isolated Indians was already changing.

> A little below this place stands the Pamunkey Indian town; where at present are the few remains of that large tribe; the rest having dwindled away through intemperance and disease. They live in little wigwams or cabins upon the river; and have a very fine tract of land of about 2,000 acres, which they are restrained from alienating by act of assembly. Their employment is chiefly hunting or fishing, for neighboring gentry. They commonly dress like the Virginians, and I have sometimes mistaken them for the lower sort of that people.

Another missionary stated that these "detached Indian families living among the white people on the banks of rivers, and on that account called River-Indians, are generally a loose set of people, like our gypsies. They make baskets, brooms, wooden spoons, dishes, &c. and sell them to the white people for victuals and clothes."

Meanwhile, those who had moved to Pennsylvania were not faring any better. The mapmaker Lewis Evans, in a brief account of Pennsylvania in 1753, wrote: "The remnants of some Nations in Subjection to the six nations & which

they have not quite extirpated wander here & There for the Sake of making ordinary wicker Baskets and Basons, within a few miles of the Town, but have no Land of Their own or fixt Habitations; What they get for their Work, they Spend in Rum & their food They beg . . ."

By 1797 the Indians' traditional relationship with their land had been completely disrupted. In that year, the anonymous author of a "Description of the Cypress Swamps in Delaware and Maryland States" noted the remains of several Indian towns and interviewed an old Indian who called himself Will Andrew. Will Andrew was a survivor of an unidentified tribe of Eastern Shore Indians.

> I once owned all this land about here. Come, said he, I will shew you, where my father lived: I walked with him about two hundred paces to an eminence about three hundred yards from a creek, where I saw a large quantity of shells. Here, said he, stamping with his foot, is the very spot where my father lived.

According to these and other accounts, it is clear that the small, scattered groups of Indians that had remained on the Eastern Shore of Maryland and Delaware were already adopting many customs of the white society. They earned some money by fishing, trapping, and hunting for their white neighbors and by making and selling baskets or wooden utensils. They used their small income to buy clothing as

A carved wooden spoon 14 1/2 inches long, typical of the simple yet functional implements made by the Nanticoke.

well as food. By the end of the century, an observer would not have been able to distinguish the lifestyle of these Indians from that of rural white families living under similar conditions in the same areas.

At first, it would not have been a severe hardship for some of these isolated Nanticoke families to remain in their traditional territory and maintain their family hunting groups. However, the natural food resources upon which they depended became increasingly scarce. Also, there was no guarantee of protection on the reservations from white settlers who wanted to take possession of their land. Where and how could they survive? Their choices were limited. They could migrate to Pennsylvania and New York to join their relatives who had left earlier, or they could try to share in the white society by becoming landowners and farmers. However, emigration no longer seemed to be a workable solution. They had heard all about the difficulties of the earlier migrant Nanticoke, who moved from one village to another in Pennsylvania, New York, and Canada during the last half of the 18th century.

By this time, whites were beginning to settle along the Eastern Shore. The shore areas were becoming more attractive to new settlers, and the colonial population was growing. By the end of the 18th century, the Nanticoke could no longer avoid contact with the newcomers. They realized that they would have to find a way to participate in the new, dominant culture.

Over the years, the Nanticoke's attitude toward the use and ownership of land gradually changed. They had tried to maintain their family hunting territory system. Between 1800 and 1830, they found that the white settlers considered them to be squatters on what had once been their land. The Nanticoke lived, as we have seen, by hunt-

A Nanticoke carrying basket made from splints of yellow pine wood.

ing, fishing, and gathering on their traditional lands, but now their lands belonged to the states of Maryland and Delaware or to the individuals who had purchased it. As the number of settlers increased and more land was cleared for agricultural use, there was not enough land available to the Nanticoke to satisfy their needs in traditional ways. One of the first steps they took in their attempt to participate in white society was to become tenants on the land. As tenants, they could work for white farmers and receive money for their labor. In some cases, they were given houses located on these farms to live in. They could grow their own gardens and crops, selling any produce they did not need for themselves. Most Nanticoke families saved every penny they could. Their goal was to get enough money to buy land of their own. By purchasing land from the whites, the Nanticoke acquired a legal deed to their property.

In taking this step, the Indians were making a significant change in their way of thinking. They were accepting the concept of private property. In the 1830s, the Nanticoke began to develop a new, self-sufficient community on the land along the Indian River in Sussex County, Delaware.

Two Nanticoke men in particular, Levin Sockum and Isaac Harman, were active in acquiring property. They were the first Nanticoke to become substantial landowners. In their wills, they would bequeath sizable parcels of land to their heirs.

Sockum was Harman's father-in-law. Harman had married Sarah, the daughter of Sockum and his wife, Eunice. Their experiences explain a great deal about the changes that the Nanticoke faced in the 19th century.

In 1837 Levin Sockum was identified for the first time in the tax assessment lists for Sussex County as a tenant farmer. He had begun accumulating money some time earlier, though. The value of Sockum's private property was set by the county assessor at $307 in 1834. Twenty years later Sockum's wealth was $1,174, which made him one of the wealthiest men in Sussex County. By this time, Sockum also owned and operated a general store at the head of Long Neck on the north shore of Indian River. It was Sockum's activities as a storekeeper that would soon bring him into conflict with the law.

Whereas the Indians had had their problems with the white community over the years, the conflicts were largely due to cultural misunderstandings. Before 1830 no overt signs of racial prejudice or hostility had been specifically directed toward the surviving Indians in Delaware. As the young United States began to experience the growing pains that would result in the Civil War, however, the Indians in Delaware, as well as blacks, became targets of white bias and animosity.

Nat Turner was a black slave who believed he had a mission to lead a slave revolt. In 1831 he led an insurrection of slaves in Southampton County, Vir-

Levin Sockum   Eunice Ridgeway Sockum

Sarah, the daughter of
Levin and Eunice Sockum, became
the wife of Isaac Harman.

Four of the eight children of Isaac and Sarah Sockum Harman.
From left, Levin T., Noah, John Wesley, and Eliza Anne.

The home of Isaac Harman and his family.

Nat Turner and his confederates planning the Southampton Insurrection of 1831, in an engraving made a few years later.

ginia, in which more than 50 whites were killed. Turner was captured and hung. Whites throughout the South feared that there would be more violent incidents. Many southern states toughened their systems of slave control. They revised the slave codes, passing excessively harsh laws to regulate the slave and free-Negro populations. The new laws legalized slave patrols, groups of armed whites who rode through the countryside at night to prevent blacks from holding meetings or congregating with each other.

The extreme fear of potential slave revolts in Delaware is shown by one particular event. Shortly after the Nat Turner rebellion, rumors of revolts spread throughout the state. People were aroused. In the fall of 1831 some men took advantage of the heightened fears by planning a phony revolt in Sussex County. They planted rumors that

the blacks would rise up in arms on the day of a general election in October. When the day came, a group of troublemakers assembled on the banks of the Nanticoke River, within sight of the town of Seaford, Delaware. They divided into two parties. One group appeared to be firing on the others, some of whom fell to the ground, pretending to be shot. Then some ran into Seaford and reported that the Negroes had landed, killed several whites, and were preparing to march through the country, bent on destruction.

"Consternation for the moment seized upon all," wrote a local editor. "The fearful ran and hid themselves in the woods, while the stout hearted flew to arms." A messenger sent to Kent County for aid arrived at the nearest election post just as a crowd had gathered and officials were tallying the votes. He shouted that 1,500 Negroes from Maryland had landed on the Nanticoke River and were already marching towards Kent County. Panic completely disrupted the election. A clerk ran off in fright, taking the ballot box with him. Although within hours it was discovered that all the reports were false, people throughout the southern counties of Delaware had believed the worst and acted accordingly.

Fear of slave rebellions brought about an immediate change in the attitude of whites toward people of other races. Laws were specifically directed against blacks, mulattoes (people of mixed black and white descent), and "people of color" (everyone who was not Caucasian). When the Delaware legislature met the following January, a bill was introduced into the House of Representatives to disarm the free Negroes and mulattoes; to prevent their holding religious or other meetings unless under the direction of respectable white people; and to forbid out-of-state free Negroes to preach or attempt to preach or hold meetings for such purposes.

The new atmosphere of racial prejudice and restriction was immediately felt by the Nanticoke and other Indian communities throughout the eastern United States. The color of their skin caused them to become targets of the new repressive legislation. In diaries, travel accounts, journals, and histories of this period, reference is continually made to their dark complexion. Robert Beverley, in his *History and Present State of Virginia*, stated: "Their Colour, when they are grown up, is a Chestnut brown and tawny. Their skin comes afterwards to harden and grow blacker." George H. Loskiel, a missionary, described their skin as a "reddish color, nearly resembling copper, but in different shades. Some are of a brown yellow, not much differing from the mulattoes." Henry Ridgely of Delaware witnessed President Andrew Jackson's interview with Black Hawk, the leader of a militant faction of the Sac tribe. Ridgely expressed his disappointment because Black Hawk was "small, unimpressive except for a fine forehead, and reminded him of some elderly Negro." In 1840, a chief of the Onondaga (one of the Six Nations of the Iroquois) tribe, whose people were being forced to emigrate from New York, stated: "Americans treat Indians so bad. They hate Indians. White men think they got better color than Indians, so they want Indians away."

Black Hawk, painted by George Catlin.

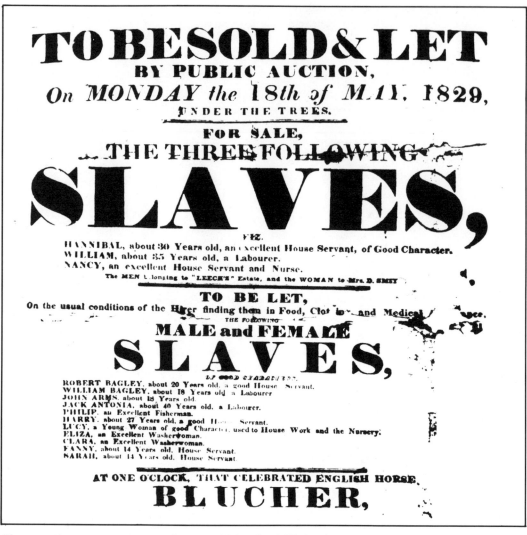

TO BE SOLD & LET

BY PUBLIC AUCTION,

On MONDAY the 18th of MAY, 1829,

UNDER THE TREES.

FOR SALE,

THE THREE FOLLOWING

SLAVES,

VIZ.

HANNIBAL, about 30 Years old, an excellent House Servant, of Good Character.
WILLIAM, about 35 Years old, a Labourer.
NANCY, an excellent House Servant and Nurse.

The MEN belonging to "LEECH'S" Estate, and the WOMAN to Mrs. D. SMIT

TO BE LET,

On the usual conditions of the Hirer finding them in Food, Clothes and Medical Attendance.

THE FOLLOWING

MALE and FEMALE

SLAVES,

OF GOOD CHARACTERS.

ROBERT BAGLEY, about 20 Years old, a good House Servant.
WILLIAM BAGLEY, about 18 Years old a Labourer
JOHN ARMS, about 18 Years old.
JACK ANTONIA, about 40 Years old, a Labourer.
PHILIP, an Excellent Fisherman.
HARRY, about 27 Years old, a good House Servant.
LUCY, a Young Woman of good Character, used to House Work and the Nursery.
ELIZA, an Excellent Washerwoman.
CLARA, an Excellent Washerwoman.
FANNY, about 14 Years old, House Servant.
SARAH, about 14 Years old, House Servant

AT ONE O'CLOCK, THAT CELEBRATED ENGLISH HORSE,

BLUCHER,

Slave auctions were a common feature of Maryland life in the early 19th century. This handbill announces the auction of three slaves. It also advertises several slaves, ages 11 and older, for "rent," as well as the sale of assorted household items.

Skin color was becoming an obsession with white Americans. In Sussex County, Delaware, most considered the Nanticoke to be a separate class of "colored" people. Although some people recognized that they were of Indian origin, many others regarded them as mulattoes.

One of Delaware's new laws prohibited the sale or loan of firearms to a Negro or mulatto. Levin Sockum, the prosperous Nanticoke landowner, ran into trouble with this law. Sockum was brought to trial for selling gunpowder to a mulatto. The customer was, in fact, his son-in-law, Isaac Harman.

Sockum admitted selling Harman the gunpowder. The prosecuting attorney, George P. Fisher, had to prove that Harman was indeed a mulatto. Fisher knew this would not be easy. He himself described Harman as a "young man, apparently about five and twenty years of age, of perfect Caucasian features, dark chestnut hair, rosy cheeks and hazel eyes." Furthermore, Fisher observed, "of all the men concerned in the trial he was the most perfect type of the pure Caucasian, and by odds the handsomest man in the court room, yet he was alleged to be a mulatto." There was considerable testimony, but not one witness could provide any information about Harman's ancestry. Finally, Fisher placed Lydia Clark, 87 years old, on the witness stand. Clark, whose physical features were indisputably Indian, was a blood relative of Harman. She was the last person to speak the Nanticoke language in Delaware.

Clark testified that before the American Revolution there had been an Irish lady named Regua (a corruption of the name Ridgeway) living on a farm in Indian River Hundred, a subdivision of Sussex County. Regua heard of a slave ship that had been driven into nearby Lewes Creek by a storm. Having recently lost one of her slaves, she decided to go to the town of Lewes to replace him. She purchased a "very tall, shapely and muscular young fellow of dark ginger-bread color," recalled Clark. The young African claimed to be a prince or chief of one of the Congo River tribes who had been sold into slavery.

Clark further testified that after a few months, Regua had married her new slave. They raised a large family,

and several of their children later intermarried with some of the remaining Nanticoke people. Harman, asserted Clark, was born to one of these couples. Regua's children were mulattoes, since they had one white parent and one black. This satisfied the court that Harman was a mulatto. Thus Sockum had indeed sold firearms to a mulatto, and he was found guilty. Sockum was fined $20 and then brought to court on a second charge, illegal possession of a gun. The court accepted testimony that Sockum too was a mulatto and fined him an additional $20.

More than a century later, it is hard to tell why Sockum had become a target. He was, after all, trying to live according to the social code of the white majority and in fact was successful at it. Perhaps he was too successful. He had become quite well-to-do by local standards and had married a wealthy white woman. In both instances, Sockum was challenging the presumed social order of Sussex County. Although what specifically prompted the accusations in the court cases may never be discovered, there are hints that Sockum may have been tried because his white neighbors were envious. The charges against him had been brought by members of the locally prominent Burton family.

Lydia Clark died less than a year after Sockum's trials. Tradition within the Nanticoke community suggests that the Burtons coerced Lydia Clark to make this prejudicial testimony against her kin. Clark's descendants maintain

In 1927 this tablet was erected in Sussex County, Delaware, to commemorate the last person to speak the Nanticoke language, Lydia Clark, who died in 1856.

to this day that she was dependent on the Burtons for food and shelter and had no choice. She was buried in an isolated part of the pine woods that bordered on the Nanticoke community. There is a crude stone marker on her grave, which the Nanticoke say was provided by the Burton family. The inscription reflects the racial prejudice and hatred of the times:

> In memory of
> Lydia Clark
> Who died Dec. 26, 1856.
> Aged about 75 years.
> The last one of the Aborigines
> Of the Country, a person of
> truth and a witness against
> the arrogant Negroes that
> assumed to be what they
> were not

For a few years after the trials, Sockum, like his son-in-law Harman, continued to increase his wealth, but he was extremely upset by the verdicts of the juries. In 1861, he sold all of his land in Sussex County to a doctor from Gloucester, New Jersey, and moved with his family to Gloucester, where his descendants remain to this day.

In New Jersey, as he had done in Delaware, Sockum opened a general store, which also offered a wide selection of women's hats and headdresses. He apparently continued to prosper, but racial prejudice continued to haunt the Sockum family. One episode concerned Eliza A. Sockum, a daughter of Levin and Eunice. Eliza was a beautiful woman with long black hair who married a successful New York City businessman. J. Perot had not met his future parents-in-law before he married Eliza. When Perot did meet Levin and Eunice Sockum, he suddenly and permanently abandoned Eliza. He charged that "his wife had been unfair to him in not being completely candid in so intimate a state as that of matrimony." Eliza suffered an emotional breakdown and died soon afterward, on September 7, 1862. Despite the unworthy conduct of her husband, the epitaph on Eliza's tombstone reflects her love for him: "Farewell to you dear husband."

Meanwhile, Isaac Harman had stayed in Delaware and prospered. The Indian River location provided him with a lucrative income. He established a very profitable business of packing and shipping soft-shell crabs. He operated another business as well, transporting lumber by boat to Millsboro, Delaware, and to New Jersey. As a young man, Isaac had earned his living by going to sea in a sailing vessel. Isaac's brother, Charles Ephraim Harman, a boatman in Philadelphia, may have helped his brother go to sea. Isaac's first land purchase was a 70-acre tract, for which he paid $250 in 1848.

The present-day Nanticoke still talk about Isaac Harman: "He seemed to have an obsession for owning property," one of them has said. "It is told that he would drive his buggy to Georgetown barefooted in order to record the purchase of another parcel of land." Harman bought more land and farm equipment to go with it.

In 1867 only two Nanticokes were identified as landowners in Indian River Hundred. They were the brothers Charles Ephraim and Isaac Harman. Most families in the area, many of them related to both Levin Sockum and Isaac Harman, were tenants on farms owned by whites and were beginning to accumulate an impressive amount of personal property. In time, these families would either inherit property or purchase their own land. The majority of these families lived in and later owned property in the area that is home to the present-day Nanticoke community.

By 1872 Isaac Harman had become one of the largest landowners in Sussex County, Delaware. His estate included most of the land bordering on the northeast shore of Indian River. The boundaries of his estate approximate the area of the Nanticoke community today.

Isaac and Sarah Sockum Harman had eight children who survived to adulthood. These eight children would inherit the land and property accumulated by their parents. Sarah Harman survived her husband. In her last will and testament of 1902, she bequeathed $1,000 to each of her children and grandchildren, a fortune at that time and place. The Harman land was divided equally among the heirs.

Even as Isaac and Charles Ephraim Harman and other Nanticoke were prospering in Delaware, many left the area. In 1855 several Nanticoke families migrated to San Francisco. Later, some of Sockum's remaining relatives moved to Detroit and Philadelphia. After the Sockum trials and these departures, though, life among the Nanticoke at Indian River settled down. They were still able to follow some of their traditional ways of securing food, but with the death of Lydia Clark, their last link to their language and much of their oral history was gone. The Sussex County Indians in the late 19th century followed the daily activities typical of many other rural agricultural communities. The men tended their crops and animals. The women and children worked in the gardens. Occasionally, Nanticoke families traveled to nearby towns to purchase necessities and sell or barter their farm produce and household wares. The Nanticoke quietly went about their own business, but their way of life was soon threatened anew. ▲

Frank Speck took this picture in the state capital after Delaware granted a charter to the Nanticoke Indian Association in 1922. The men, all Nanticoke, are, from left: *Fred Clark, Assistant Chief E. Lincoln Harman, Chief William Russel Clark, Warren Wright, and Isaac Johnson. Gladys Tantaquidgeon,* foreground, *a Mohegan Indian, was Speck's student and assistant.*

STRUGGLE
FOR
RECOGNITION

The guilty verdicts against Levin Sockum cemented the racial status and classification of the Nanticoke. Now it was official: the white population in Delaware would treat the Nanticoke in the same manner as it treated blacks. This discriminatory treatment intensified after the Civil War. In the Middle Atlantic states, as in the Deep South, blacks and Indians went to segregated schools, prayed in separate churches, lived in distinct neighborhoods, and did not associate with whites in day-to-day activities. As far as the state was concerned, the Indians were indistinguishable from the larger minority population. During the late 19th century, the Nanticoke struggled continuously for separate recognition as Indians.

This ambiguous identity of the Nanticoke was most sharply reflected in continued controversy over schooling. Delaware, like many other states, maintained a segregated public school system, with separate schools for blacks and for whites. (This would continue until 1965.) No additional facilities were available to Indians.

In 1875 Delaware passed "An Act to Tax Colored Persons for the Support of Their Schools." This legislation levied an assessment of 30 cents for every $100 of property on all Negroes and colored persons. This money was to be used to build and maintain their separate schools. Insensitive to the Indian population, the legislators classified the Nanticoke, along with other nonwhite people, as colored persons. Thus the Indians were required to pay this tax, and Nanticoke children would be legally required to attend schools for blacks.

The Nanticoke were indignant. To submit to this legislation would undermine their long struggle to maintain their separate Indian identity. Until then, they had maintained their own separate educational system. It was simple, but it was independent and their own. Usually the Nanticoke children had been taught in their homes by a traveling preacher from Lewes, Delaware. At times Samuel B. Norwood's barn served as a school, and sometimes the church was used.

White intolerance and prejudice had relegated blacks to the lowest rung of the social ladder. If the Nanticoke accepted the tax imposed by the legislature of Delaware, they felt they would lose their own distinct identity and, in effect, be accepting the status accorded to Negroes. The Nanticoke decided to resist in order to survive ethnically and culturally. They organized and hired an attorney. They pressured local politicians to exempt them from this tax, with the understanding that they would erect and support their own school.

Out of this active protest against the Act of 1875 developed a new legal identity for the Nanticoke, known as the Incorporated Body. On March 10, 1881, the Delaware General Assembly formally recognized the Incorporated Body and exempted its members and their families from the Act of 1875. Their new legal status makes it possible for the Nanticoke to function as a unit, in much the same way as a business organization. They were permitted to build and maintain at their own expense two schools, which would be separate from the white and black schools. Indian children between the ages of 7 and 21 could attend their own schools.

Although this was a major victory for the Nanticoke community, the specific terms "Indian" and "Nanticoke" were not mentioned in the legislation creating the Incorporated Body. Instead, the law simply stated that this organization would be incorporated as "The Indian River School District for A

Certain Class of Colored Persons." The assembly had deliberately avoided identifying the Indians living in Delaware as Indians.

Nevertheless, the Nanticoke had successfully achieved their goal of separate schools for their children. With membership dues and donations from the Nanticoke community, the Incorporated Body began immediately to build two one-room schoolhouses on land donated by its members. They were called the Hollyville School and the Warwick School. Each school had one white teacher whose salary was paid by the Incorporated Body.

The law of 1881 did not legally resolve questions about the racial identity of the Nanticoke. They were simply recognized as "a special class"—that is, not black—of "colored" or nonwhite people. In 1903 the Incorporated Body and its attorney went before the Delaware assembly to demand that the phrase "a certain class of colored persons" be changed. They were Indians and they wanted to be called Indians!

In its next session, the assembly passed a law entitled "An Act to Better Establish the Identity of a Race of People Known as the Offspring of the Nanticoke Indians." This act was direct and to the point: "The descendants of the Nanticoke Indians shall hereafter be recognized as such within the State of Delaware." This law was the first legislation to recognize and acknowledge the Nanticoke living in Delaware.

In 1916 a citizens' committee in Delaware surveyed the school system throughout the state and found most of the schools to be terribly inadequate. With financial support from the Dupont family, the leading industrialists in the state, approximately two-thirds of the schools in Delaware were rebuilt. In Indian River Hundred, where most of the Nanticoke lived, new schools were built for blacks and whites. The Delaware Board of Education also planned to build schools "for use by the children of the people called Moors." "Moors," a term sometimes used to describe the Nanticoke, was also the name given to another small community of Indians (some of whom were related to the Nanticoke) living in Cheswold, Delaware. When the new school program was completed in the 1920s, Delaware had separate schools for blacks, whites, Indians (the Nanticoke), and Moors (the Cheswold people).

Then local authorities violated the 1881 law by admitting non-Indian children to the Hollyville and Warwick schools. The Nanticoke, protesting this violation and once again asserting their Indian identity, immediately withdrew their children from the schools. They built a one-room, wood-frame schoolhouse which became known as the Indian Mission School. Nanticoke children would continue to go to this school until the late 1960s.

The Nanticoke's determination to maintain their Indian identity also re-

The Warwick School

The Harmony African Methodist Church

sulted in their maintaining separate churches. During the 19th century, there had been considerable missionary activity on the Eastern Shore by the Methodist church. Prior to 1867 the many Nanticoke who were Methodists had attended their own church, which was served by a traveling pastor. After this building was destroyed by fire, a new church was built, and a white pastor was sent to serve the Indian congregation. The congregation objected and requested that an Indian pastor be sent to serve them. When a new minister was hired, part of the congregation withdrew, claiming the man was a Negro. In 1888 the dissenters began holding services in private homes. They soon constructed a new church, known today as the Indian Mission United Methodist Church. The church that the

dissenters left became known as the Harmony African Methodist Episcopal Church. The dissenting group consisted for the most part of the same individuals who had pushed for separate schools and initiated the "Incorporated Body" act of 1881. The gap within the Nanticoke community was becoming wider. Most Nanticoke continue to this day to attend the Indian Mission United Methodist Church.

As the Nanticoke and other Indian tribes in the East were struggling to retain their identity, American anthropologists at the end of the 19th century were studying the better-known tribes further west. They hoped to "salvage" artifacts and folklore before the Indians' way of life disappeared forever, which they assumed would be soon. Some anthropologists became aware of the small

Indian communities scattered throughout the eastern United States and decided to try to salvage their artifacts and folklore, too. Over the years, the Nanticoke were visited by three anthropologists.

In 1898 William H. Babcock became the first professional anthropologist to visit the Nanticoke community. After a few days' stay, Babcock rejected the racially biased opinion of local whites and willingly identified these people as Indians. He published a brief report about the Nanticoke in the *American Anthropologist*. He described their successful farming activities, the racial hostility

that had resulted in separate schools and churches, and the social isolation of the community. Babcock concluded that the Nanticoke should not be neglected any longer. "They ask no help, being very well able to take care of themselves," he observed. "But the anthropologic world may brighten matters a little for them by showing that in their struggle for individual existence they have at last become visible to the scientific eye."

In 1908 the Nanticoke were visited by Mark R. Harrington. Harrington was working for George G. Heye, an avid collector of Indian artifacts who would

Nanticokes demonstrating the use of a corn mortar and corn sheller.

soon acquire so many that he would found the Museum of the American Indian in New York City. Harrington, buying objects for Heye's collection, stayed with the Nanticoke for two or three days. He purchased a corn sheller, a corn mortar and pestle, oak-splint baskets, and an eel trap but did not report or publish anything about his visit.

Perhaps the most influential anthropologist to study the Nanticoke was Frank G. Speck, a professor of anthropology at the University of Pennsylvania. While most American anthropologists of the time were studying Indian tribes in the western United States, Speck was visiting many of the forgotten Indian communities in the eastern United States. He realized that many people questioned the racial identity of these people because they did not "look" or "act" like Indians. He recognized that Indians who had spent almost three centuries adjusting to white customs could not be expected to retain their earlier way of life. These Indian descendants did have their own distinctive culture, but it was a culture that had undergone significant change since their first contact with European explorers and settlers. "Native architecture, clothing, utensils, furnishings, weapons, vehicles, amusements, ornaments, fishing, hunting and trapping methods did not die out," Speck argued. "They changed." Only through personal acquaintance with, and firsthand observation of, present-day Indians could these surviving traits be studied.

Speck, who had read Babcock's report on the Nanticoke, first visited the Sussex County community in 1911. He was particularly interested in the activities and tools involved in the production of corn. The Nanticoke used suckering canes, cornhusking pegs, corn shellers, and large log corncribs to produce, process, and store corn. The suckering cane was a crooked stick of oak with a natural bend forming a handle. The men pulled the surplus sprouts out of the cornhills with the suckering cane as they went through the fields. The sharp end of the cane was also used to poke holes in the hills for planting the seeds of corn.

When the corn was ready to be harvested, the men would go into the fields and husk the ears, using a cornhusking peg, while the plants were still standing. After the corn was husked, children would gather the cobs in large baskets. The corn cobs were then stored in the log corncribs. The corn sheller

A suckering cane, an oak branch that is naturally crooked, was used to pull unwanted corn shoots out of the earth. The pointed end was used to poke holes in which corn kernels would be planted.

Making an eel pot (trap). The late Elwood Wright, a Nanticoke crafts worker, wove splints of yellow pine wood around a wooden mold held horizontally in a stand. As he worked, he turned the mold with one hand and wove with the other.

was a section of a hollow log with branches inserted in holes across the base. Cobs of dried corn were placed in the sheller and pounded with poles. The pounding removed the dried kernels from the cobs. The kernels fell beneath the branches at the base, ready to be stored in baskets or ground to make cornmeal.

Nearly every Nanticoke family possessed a mortar and pestle to pound their corn into grits or flour. A coarse cornmeal dough called pone was used to make certain foods of Indian origin. Among these were the ash cake and johnnycake. An ash cake was a disk of corn dough, about six inches wide, wrapped in large, damp leaves and placed in the ashes of a dying fire. Johnnycake was made of corn dough spread upon an oak board. The johnnycake board was tilted on its side in front of an open fire until the cake turned brown.

Also of interest to Speck were the fishing methods of the Nanticoke. The Nanticoke obtained much of their food from the Indian River, using the same devices and methods for catching fish

as had their ancestors. Their fishing equipment included eelpots, fishnets, netting needles, mesh sticks, and fykes (bag-shaped nets used to trap a fish). Speck spent many hours in the company of the Nanticoke men, observing and recording their traditional activities. Elwood Wright was one of the last Nanticoke who knew how to make baskets and eelpots from oak splints. The eelpot was made from either pine or oak strips about half an inch to an inch wide. The horizontal strips were woven one over, one under, the long vertical strips. Weaving began several inches from the ends of the vertical strips. Each horizontal row was placed above the preceding row. When the weaving was complete, the unwoven ends of the vertical strips would be bent inward. The eelpot was placed on its side in the water near the shore. Stones were placed inside the eelpot so that it would sink to the bottom. The eels entered the basket through an opening at one end. At the other end, the bent strips kept the eels or fish from escaping.

Speck was also very interested in Indian folklore. The Nanticoke had many

Chief William Russel Clark became a close friend of anthropologist Frank Speck, who took this picture in 1922.

Frank G. Speck, the anthropologist who visited the Nanticoke over a period of many years.

interesting beliefs concerning medical practices, the weather, and other aspects of everyday life.

Their medical folk practices could protect or cure many ills. They wore an eelskin around the part of the body affected by arthritis to reduce pain. They covered cuts with cobwebs until they healed. They rubbed the cut surface of a prickly pear on warts to remove them. They tied the skin of a blacksnake around the waist to cure a backache. They wore a necklace of deerskin to prevent whooping cough or kernels from an ear of red corn to prevent nosebleed.

The Nanticoke depended on natural signs to predict the weather. Wild geese flying overhead meant that a strong wind was coming. Crows or blackbirds landing in a field showed that rain was on the way. The whippoorwill's first cry in the spring was the sign that it was time to plant corn.

There were also special omens and signs that meant that the viewer would experience a disappointment. A black animal seen crossing one's path at the beginning of a venture was a sign of bad luck. The cooing of the mourning dove indicated the direction in which one's lover could be found.

Frank Speck continued to visit the Nanticoke over the years, and he became quite friendly with William Russel Clark. Russel Clark, as he was called, was a descendant of Lydia Clark, who had testified at Levin Sockum's trial, and was particularly knowledgeable about the tribe's history and culture. In 1921 Russel Clark was elected chief of the Nanticoke people. At the time, the schism between the two church congregations was becoming more intense, and Delaware was placing non-Indian students in the Nanticoke schools. Since they had legally incorporated in

1881, the Nanticoke had maintained their own schools and churches in order to preserve their distinctiveness and separation from the black population, but by the 1920s very few people in the community remembered the importance of the Incorporated Body. Chief Russel Clark recognized that the racial integrity of the community was being threatened again and consulted Speck.

As Clark and Speck saw it, the traditionalists in the Nanticoke community needed authorization to assert their Indian identity legally. Speck, after considerable deliberation, consulted with an attorney. The lawyer suggested that the Nanticoke form a corporation and obtain a charter from the state of Delaware. On February 24, 1922, the Nanticoke Indian Association received a charter of incorporation from Delaware. Clark was reelected chief, and E. Lincoln Harman became assistant chief. Clark's power was now enhanced because he had legal authority as the chief executive officer of the corporation.

Speck had not imposed his own opinions on the Nanticoke. He had acted only as their adviser and intermediary with the non-Indian world. After the Nanticoke community representatives agreed to the formation of an independent organization, Speck turned all matters over to the association's newly elected officers.

One of the major objectives of the Nanticoke Indian Association was to renew interest in the old Indian traditions. Frank Speck, who had worked for many years with other Algonkian peoples in Canada and the northeastern United States, would help them realize this goal. The Nanticoke no longer retained their native language and practiced little of their traditional way of life. Speck was impressed with their intense interest in their Indian heritage. He taught his friends the steps to simple dances and words to songs. He helped them make costumes, strings of beads, and feather headdresses.

After they had begun to learn some Algonkian traditions, the members of the Nanticoke Indian Association decided to hold a festival. This festival resembled the traditional campfire powwows of most Algonkian tribes, with singing, dancing, and eating, and became an annual get-together. Nanticoke family members would drive from scattered locations in Delaware and neighboring states to come to the powwow held at Thanksgiving time every year.

The Nanticoke realized that these songs, dances, and costumes were not part of their own tribal heritage. They wanted only to strengthen their spirit of being Indian, and to do so by borrowing some traditional customs from other, related tribes. Unfortunately, the local white community was unsympathetic. Very few whites living in Delaware in the 1920s knew anything about an Indian powwow. Headlines in local newspapers ridiculed the idea. "Delaware Redskins Revive Old Tribal Custom for Thanksgiving Celebration" and "Nanticokes Following Custom of Tribal Ancestors Give Thanks with

Weird Dances" were typical of whites' reactions.

Despite the lack of understanding of some of their white neighbors, the Nanticoke continued to hold powwows for about a dozen years. The powwows were discontinued in the 1930s, when people could not afford the cost of gasoline. Gasoline rationing during the Second World War continued to make travel difficult.

Speck continued to visit the Nanticoke until the death of Chief Russel Clark in 1928. The anthropologist and the chief had shared a rare, close friendship. Speck later wrote that "the lure of Indian River passed away with him."

In the 1930s another white American, the historian Clinton A. Weslager, became interested in the Nanticoke community. He visited the Indian River community, became friendly with Lincoln Harman, and wrote articles and a book about the Nanticoke, published in the 1940s.

Speck did not return to Indian River until 1942, after an absence of 14 years. When he returned, he found that there had been considerable change. New roads made travel to other towns and cities easier. Grade school attendance was compulsory, and the children were bringing many of the Nanticoke into the mainstream of white society. "It was hard to believe at first," Speck remarked after driving through the community. "It seemed that only imagination could forge links with the past." But closer observance showed that traditions had not been completely lost. Several young men were still trapping animals to supplement the food available from other sources. Indian customs still dictated much of the social behavior. Traditional domestic utensils and recipes were still being used in many households.

In the 1940s the Nanticoke would once again have to struggle to assert their Indian identity. Ironically, their battle resulted from the efforts of their young men to enlist in the United States Army during World War II. At that time, the armed forces were segregated by race. Blacks and Indians each served in their own units. In Delaware, as elsewhere, draft boards and military administrators had problems classifying young men who claimed Indian descent. The Indian rights of the Nanticoke men who had been inducted were recognized by Delaware law. These rights were disregarded by military authorities, who classified the Nanticoke as Negroes. As a result, two young Nanticoke men who had been drafted were stationed with black soldiers in the South, although they had requested classification as Indians. The Nanticoke called upon Weslager for assistance. W. Berl, state director of the Delaware Selective Service, had no problem in classifying the Nanticoke as Indian, but as he informed Weslager, the final classification of the two soldiers was up to the army. Weslager contacted the adjutant general of the United States Army in June 1942 and requested information about the proper procedures for transferring the two Nanticoke soldiers to either white or American Indian units. He also asked how the Indian

QUILTING PARTY

I can remember having what we used to call a quilting party. I would use scrap cotton materials I had left over from making the children's clothes. We used only cotton materials in making a quilt so it could be washed and you didn't have to worry about it shrinking.

In those days, the chicken feed came in bags, cotton bags. Some were plain, some were print, and some were striped. We would rip the side seam, and wash it to get the smell of feed out of them. After using these bags to make clothes, tea towels, and aprons, I would use the leftover scraps for quilting material.

I would have to cut the scraps into squares about four inches square. The next job was to get the ironing board and the flat irons out. Of course in those days we didn't have any electricity. We had flat irons that we heated on the wood stove.

All of this work was done during the day if you had the time; otherwise you worked on it at night. We didn't have TV for entertainment then and we really didn't have the time for it. Farming was much harder work then than it is now. We used mules instead of tractors and we had to pump all our water for the chickens. So it was up early in the morning and work all day until dark. In the winter it was different and this was when we would work on our quilts.

Back to the quilting squares. I would sew these squares together by hand until I had enough to cover a full bed. I would mix the patterns and colors so it would have a pretty design. I only worked on this in my spare time. Sometimes it would take half the winter just to get the squares sewn together. Mostly I would work on this after the children were in bed. Since it was winter I sometimes stayed up till eleven or twelve o'clock.

Once I had all the squares together I would invite the other women for a quilting party. I would have the frame all set up when they came. The frame was where you put the squares on top of the lining, which was probably an old worn-out blanket. The back was made of plain colored feed bags sewn together. The frame held it all tight. You sat in chairs, maybe three women to each side, and sewed by hand all three layers together. This way the layers did not separate and you had a nice flat blanket. About the end of winter the quilt would be done.

Told by Patience Harman

status of future Nanticoke conscripts could be preserved. Weslager received an answer from Brigadier General H. B. Lewis, adjutant general of the War Department, at the end of July.

"With regard to race, there are two categories within the Army, white and colored," Lewis wrote. His letter continued: "Members of the Negro race are assigned to colored units. All other distinct races are assigned to white units. Individuals of races with distinguishable Negro characteristics acquired through intermixture with that race are assigned to colored units. Under this policy, an Indian may be assigned as an individual to a white unit or he may be assigned to a company or regiment made up entirely of Indians, that company or regiment being a component part of a white regiment or division."

As to the two men from Indian River, the local draft board in Georgetown, Delaware, had classified them as colored. To prevent any future mishaps, Weslager was informed, the registrar at the local draft board would classify the inductee as belonging to whatever race he claimed. If an inductee was registered as being of a race other than that he claimed, the matter had to be referred to the state director of the Selective Service. When a similar misunderstanding occurred the following year, the young man involved was immediately transferred out of the black unit into a white unit.

The legal identity of the Nanticoke was called into question again after World War II. Once again the issue concerned educational facilities for "colored" people. As we have seen, Delaware, like many other states, had separate schools for whites and blacks. In the Nanticoke area there were also separate schools for Indians. Although the separate schools of the Nanticoke helped them preserve their Indian status, the quality of education was vastly inferior to that in schools for whites.

In Delaware there were no high schools for Indians. The Nanticoke, trying still to preserve their Indian identity and status, refused to send their children to the high schools for blacks and were not allowed to send them to the high schools for whites. There were, therefore, very few Nanticokes who were high school graduates. One way to get around this predicament was to send the Nanticoke students to Haskell Institute in Lawrence, Kansas, one of four all-Indian schools run by the Bureau of Indian Affairs (BIA), the federal agency responsible for administering the government's Indian policy.

Admitting a student to Haskell required the signature of the authorities who represented the government on many of the federal Indian reservations. But the Delaware Nanticoke, of course, were not living on a reservation. Several Nanticoke parents called on Weslager to help them solve this problem. Weslager wrote to Haskell Institute and the BIA, which administered the reservations as well as the Indian schools.

Some years earlier Frank Speck had similarly intervened on behalf of several Nanticoke students, and they had been

Some of the log corn cribs on the Harman family farm.

approved for enrollment to Haskell Institute. In fact, Speck had gotten an official of the BIA, Willard W. Beatty, to visit the Nanticoke. Thus, there was a precedent for this new appeal.

"I realize that they are not an organized tribe in our sense of the word and therefore do not have a Reservation Principal, Field Agent or Social Worker," Beatty now acknowledged to Weslager. "In this particular instance, an application signed by the school teacher and, I would hope, countersigned by yourself would be considered adequate." Nanticoke students continued to attend Haskell, and the biracial educational system continued to function legally in Sussex County until 1965, a year after Congress had passed the landmark Civil Rights Act, which required, among other things, a single, racially integrated school system in every state.

From 1855 to 1965 the identity of the Nanticoke was repeatedly questioned, and they had to use legal means to define their identity officially or lose their distinctive status forever. Their efforts to maintain their ethnic identity in the face of repeated attempts to classify them as black became more intense during this period. Yet the Nanticoke succeeded despite the continued threats to the social solidarity of their community. While most of these problems were resolved by the Nanticoke, some required help from empathetic individuals outside of the community. ▲

Nanticoke children playing a game called "bear in the ring" were photographed by Frank Speck.

RENEWAL

The lifestyle of the Nanticoke Indians today resembles that of their white neighbors. There has been a great deal of change in their culture since their first contact with Captain John Smith, but the Nanticoke community still living at Indian River in Delaware is a vivid demonstration that some of the Indian tribes in the eastern United States—although they have lost much of their traditional way of life—have survived. The Nanticoke want to continue as a distinct ethnic group. Today's Nanticoke people, like their ancestors, have many challenges to meet as they claim their rightful place in American society. They know the problems they will have to face to preserve their Nanticoke Indian Association and instill and strengthen in their children concern for their Indian heritage.

In the years following World War II, involvement in the Nanticoke Indian Association declined. Many of the older members of the association, those people who had been most interested in the old traditions, had died. Their deaths deprived the tribe of valuable leadership and role models for the younger Nanticoke to follow. Frank Speck died in 1950. For several decades, his research and periodic visits to the community had sustained considerable interest among the Nanticoke in their heritage. It would be 25 years before there was renewed research about the Nanticoke. Over the years, the younger members of the tribe became even less interested, and the association's membership and activities steadily declined.

The Nanticoke Indian Association nevertheless continued to hold meetings through the 1950s. After Chief Russel Clark died, he was succeeded by his sons Ferdinand and Robert. In late May 1932, another son, Charles C. Clark, became chief. On June 27, 1952, when Charles Clark was reelected, the members discussed the possibility of reviving the powwows. Nothing more was done, however. On December 22, 1952, while Charles Clark was still chief, the Nanticoke Indian Association held its last official meeting. It remained legally in existence, although no more official meetings were held.

The one major issue that seems to have had the greatest effect on the Nanticoke during the 1950s and 1960s concerned desegregation of the public schools. In 1954 the Supreme Court unanimously held in *Brown* v. *Board of Education of Topeka, Kansas* that racial segregation in the public schools violated the constitutional rights of minority groups. In Delaware, as in most states that had maintained biracial educational systems, desegregation did not come easily or quickly. Many Nanticoke parents continued to send their high-school-aged children to Haskell Institute. By 1961, however, the previously all-white Millsboro High School in Sussex County was admitting both Indian and black students. On September 5, 1962, the Indian Mission School formally closed its doors. The building itself continued in use as a community center.

On April 13, 1971, Chief Charles Clark was killed in a farm accident. He had been chief for almost 40 years. It seemed that with his death the Nanticoke tribe and the association would cease to exist. It probably would have, except for a request made to the Nanticoke by other Indian tribes.

The Coalition of Eastern Native Americans had been formed by representatives of tribes from Maine to Florida. The coalition's purpose was to help tribes in the eastern United States organize in order to receive and administer funds that the federal government had designated for American Indians. The Nanticoke were asked to join the coalition. On January 14, 1975, several younger Nanticoke met in the old Indian Mission School building, and the Nanticoke Indian Association came back to life.

Kenneth S. Clark, son of the pre-

Chief Charles C. Clark, in his office, right, *and wearing his ceremonial outfit.*

A classroom in a school for blacks, 1935. Delaware was one of the states that maintained segregated schools until after the Supreme Court ruled in 1954 that segregated facilities violated the Constitution. Public schools in the Nanticoke's area of the state began to be desegregated in the early 1960s.

vious tribal leader, was elected chief. The association members agreed to meet monthly. They decided that the officers elected by the tribe would serve for two years.

Kenneth Clark had been living in Philadelphia, where he was a police officer. After his father's death a few years earlier, he had returned to Indian River to manage the family business. "Until my father died, I never really realized the importance of knowing your heritage," he said. "After he did die, and I became chief of the tribe, people started coming up and asking me about the history and traditions of the Nanticokes, and I wished I had gotten more of the history from my father

and grandfather while they were still around."

The study and preservation of the history and culture of the Nanticoke became a major objective of the newly elected leaders. Kenneth Clark has continued to be reelected chief into the late 1980s.

Before 1970 the Indian policy of the federal government did not directly involve the Nanticoke. Many tribes, mostly in the West, had "trust" status. These tribes were officially recognized as having a nation-to-nation relationship directly with the federal government. As a result, trust-status tribes received services, such as health benefits, education, and economic devel-

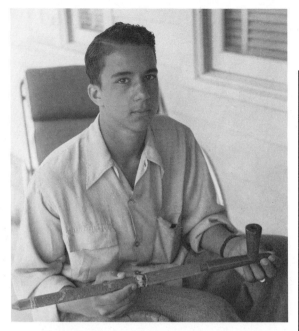

Kenneth Clark, the 15-year-old son of Chief Charles Clark, on the porch of the family home in 1946. He holds a traditional pipe used for smoking on ceremonial occasions. Kenneth Clark became chief of the Nanticoke in 1975.

Home of Chief Charles Clark

opment aid, directly from the federal government, and not from the states. Trust status Indians lived on land, usually reservations, that was legally held in trust for the tribes by the federal government. They were guaranteed certain protections and self-government by the U.S. government. These legal relationships and obligations had been worked out in a succession of treaties, largely during the 19th century. No other ethnic or racial group of the American population has had this unique relationship and these historic rights.

Like many other tribes in the eastern United States, the Nanticoke were never officially recognized as a trust status tribe. Without this unique relationship, the Nanticoke have not been eligible to receive any benefits or services provided through the Bureau of Indian Affairs. Deprived of their right

to such benefits in the areas of health, education, and economic development, the Nanticoke have successfully relied on their self-sufficient character to meet the needs of their people.

The rejuvenation of the Nanticoke Indian Association made it possible for the Nanticoke to get funds from other federal programs. The Department of Labor, for example, has a Division of Indian and Native American Programs that provides employment and training to American Indians who are unemployed, underemployed, or economically disadvantaged. Some funds for these purposes were authorized by the Comprehensive Employment and Training Act (CETA). The Nanticoke received CETA funds in 1979 to create summer jobs and provide training for high school students and unemployed members of the tribe. One Nanticoke was hired to be the full-time administrator of these activities. Under the CETA program, people were hired and trained to renovate the old Indian Mission School building, which was converted into the Nanticoke Indian Center. In addition to housing the CETA office, the Indian Center provided space for arts and crafts programs, conferences, senior citizen activities, and the monthly meetings of the Nanticoke Indian Association.

Meanwhile, the land along the Indian River in Sussex County has become quite valuable. The United States experienced several decades of prosperity following the Second World War. Automobile sales skyrocketed, and gasoline was inexpensive. Many people became able to afford second homes, and waterfront sites were in demand for vacations. Some of the Nanticoke leased or sold their land for the construction of summer cottages. Choice property along the shores of Indian River was the first such real estate to be sold. It is ironic that this isolated area, once disdained and avoided by whites, has become a haven for summer vacationers and weekend tourists. Waterfront property now sells at very high prices and is becoming quite scarce. Increasingly, tracts of land near or within the Nanticoke community are being purchased. The new developments range from Oak Orchard West, a mobile-home park, to chic, new private communities, such as Gull Point. The private developments limit public access to the waterfront. What was once a public beach where the Nanticoke used to fish and swim is now posted with such signs as "No Trespassing," "No Camping," "Reserved Parking," and "No Fishing." Only the sea gulls are free to roam the beach.

Until recently, the remaining land in the community had stayed under the ownership of Nanticoke families. This land had been used primarily for agriculture. Over the years, these farms were divided and subdivided into smaller and smaller parcels for married children and their families. These smaller tracts of land cannot be farmed efficiently using large-scale commercial techniques because of the high cost of equipment, fertilizer, and irrigation.

Consequently, many Nanticoke lease their land to other farmers who work combined tracts, or they sharecrop on additional property, paying part of their harvest as rent. Others farm only as a secondary source of income, usually keeping only small vegetable gardens that provide vegetables to sell to summer tourists.

The primary source of income of most Nanticokes is provided by skilled labor and crafts. An increasing number are high school graduates, and several have gone on to college. Today most have entered blue-collar and white-collar occupations. But at the same time as they have entered the mainstream of the American economy, the Nanticoke have showed increased concern for their Indian heritage.

At the time the Nanticoke Indian Association was revived, it had been virtually defunct for 20 years. Kenneth Clark and the new tribal council elected in 1975 reestablished and encouraged exploration of the Nanticoke heritage. The 1970s was a time of renewed ethnic identity in the United States. As people of every background began taking a new interest in their customs and history, the Nanticoke began anew to explore their own past.

One effort that focused on their cultural history was the Nanticoke Indian Heritage project of 1977. The association had sought and received funds from Delaware to make an inventory of the cultural resources of the community. The tribe identified structures, such as churches, schools, homes, and log corncribs, that had been relevant to its growth and development. As a result of this survey, nine buildings in the Indian River area were placed on the National Register of Historic Places.

Each year since 1979, the Nanticoke have held a powwow. Some 30,000 people, non-Indians and Indians of all tribes, arrive on the first weekend in September for this major public event. As in earlier years, the powwow reaffirms the sense of community and spirit among the Nanticoke and expresses to the outside world their intention to survive as a tribe in the modern world. The powwow is an Indian cultural celebration. It is a time for sharing their heritage; getting to know each other as individuals, families, and peoples; developing mutual respect, trust, and honor. Many of the dances are borrowed from the common heritage of tribes across the country. The drumming and chants, too, are shared with other Indian groups. But the Toe Dance is special; only the Nanticoke can do the Toe Dance. Regardless of their tribal origin, the music and dance carry a message of beauty and spirit. For when American Indians dance, they are expressing their most sacred beliefs, deepest feelings, and strongly held values.

The annual Homecoming of the Nanticoke also helps to bring the community closer together. In day-to-day life in modern society, there is a gap between the elderly and the young members of the Nanticoke tribe. The Homecoming is an opportunity to bring

(continued on page 89)

THE MODERN POWWOW

The traditional powwow was a solemn occasion, with prayers and sacred songs, drumming and rattles, singing and dancing. Algonkian Indians held a powwow to cure diseases or ward off evil spirits. Some tribes used the powwow as a dance feast or celebration before a council meeting, war expedition, or hunt. Modern Indian powwows have an entirely different meaning and purpose. The Nanticoke powwow is a social gathering with singing, dancing, and eating. It lasts for several days, and Indians of other tribes as well as non-Indian spectators are invited. There is also a commercial aspect to the powwow. Nanticoke craftspeople and those from visiting tribes have booths where they offer a wide variety of products for sale.

(continued from page 84)

these groups together. It is also a time for members of the tribe who have moved away from the community to come home to see old friends and renew family ties.

The Homecoming dates from the early years of the 20th century, even before the powwow began. It has always been held on the second Sunday in October. In the morning a service is held at the Indian Mission Church. Afterwards there is an outdoor potluck type of feast. For historic reasons, a feast came to be included in the Homecoming. The same state laws that before the 1960s required separate schools for whites and blacks also required separate eating places. Racial prejudice against all people of nonwhite appearance prevented the Nanticoke from being served in public restaurants and diners while traveling from neighboring cities. Knowing that many of their people would arrive hungry, the Nanticoke prepared large amounts of food to share with friends and relatives. Even though segregation in public places has ended, the afternoon-long feast remains a vital part of Homecoming. It reminds the Nanticoke of the struggle of their ancestors and provides a warm social event at the same time.

The success of the powwow made it possible to realize another dream of the Nanticoke. In 1975, when the Nanticoke Indian Association was revived,

Ceremonial costumes from the early Thanksgiving powwows are displayed in the Nanticoke Indian Museum.

the idea of founding their own museum was briefly discussed. The inventory taken for the Indian Heritage project in 1977 seemed a successful first step. In 1979 the members decided that proceeds from the sale of food, arts and crafts, and T-shirts at the powwows would be used to create the Nanticoke Indian Museum. On June 25, 1980, the state of Delaware gave an abandoned school building to the Nanticoke Indian Association for this purpose. After many months of work on the building by volunteers, the museum opened to the public in the spring of 1985. Several members of the tribe have donated their own family treasures along with objects found in the fields. The museum collections include artifacts, books, regalia, and other mementos of the past. There are baskets of many forms and wooden farm tools and household items of the late 19th and early 20th centuries. The most impressive display in the museum is the large case of mannequins dressed in the powwow costumes of the 1920s and 1930s—the first powwow costumes, made under the supervision of Frank Speck. There is also a large reference collection of books, pamphlets, and articles about the Nanticoke and other American Indian tribes, many donated by friends and neighbors of the Nanticoke.

What does the future hold for the Nanticoke tribe? When other people attempted to define who they were, the Nanticoke responded with a strong

Charles Wright was among those who painted, plastered, wired, and otherwise renovated the old Harman School building to turn it into the Nanticoke Indian Museum.

This 1946 photo shows why Indian River Bay, Delaware, home of the Nanticoke since the early 19th century, attracted vacationers whose summer cottages and private beach clubs now line the shores.

spirit and maintained their identity in the face of cultural oppression. Today they have the responsibility of keeping their own tribal customs as well as adapting to the modern world. The racial and cultural prejudices that were directed by white society at the Nanticoke in the past resulted in a lack of communication between the two peoples. The Nanticoke have assumed the responsibility of breaking down these racial and cultural barriers, too.

The Nanticoke of tomorrow will face these same responsibilities. The temp-tations of the non-Indian society reach out to the Nanticoke children, who enjoy the same leisure activities as non-Indian children. Movie theaters, video games, television, and radio bring the outside world much closer today than in the past. Like Chief Kenneth Clark, most of today's Nanticoke elders had to be recalled to their heritage. The elders know that most non-Indian children can go through life without having to prove their identity. They know they must preserve their heritage, or it will be lost to their descendants forever. ▲

BIBLIOGRAPHY

Manakee, Harold R. *Indians of Early Maryland; A Book on Maryland Life*. Baltimore: Maryland Historical Society, 1959.

Porter, Frank W., III. *Maryland Indians: Yesterday and Today*. Baltimore: Maryland Historical Society, 1983.

————. *A Photographic Survey of Indian River Community*. Millsboro, DE: Indian Mission Church, 1977.

————. *In Pursuit of the Past: An Anthropological and Bibliographic Guide to Maryland and Delaware*. Metuchen, NJ: The Scarecrow Press, 1986.

————. "Strategies for Survival: The Nanticoke Indians in a Hostile World." *Ethnohistory* 26 (Winter 1979): 325–345.

Speck, Frank G. "The Nanticoke Community of Delaware." *Contributions from the Museum of the American Indian, Heye Foundation* 2 (4). New York: Museum of the American Indian, 1915.

Weslager, Clinton A. *The Nanticoke Indians—Past and Present*. Newark, DE: University of Delaware Press, 1983.

THE NANTICOKE AT A GLANCE

TRIBE *Nanticoke*

CULTURE AREA *Middle Atlantic*

GEOGRAPHY *Maryland-Delaware Coastal Plain*

LINGUISTIC FAMILY *Algonquian*

CURRENT POPULATION *1,000*

FIRST CONTACT *John Smith, English, 1608*

FEDERAL STATUS *nonrecognized*

GLOSSARY

Algonkian The Indian people living in northeastern United States and east-central Canada whose languages are related and who share numerous cultural characteristics.

Algonquian The languages spoken by most Indian tribes in northeastern North America; the languages of the Algonkian people.

Archaic Period The way of life of American Indians from about 10,000 to 3,000 years ago, following the end of the Pleistocene. It generally involved hunting and gathering and was characterized by the invention of improved weapons, seasonal migrations, and the use of fire.

artifact Any object made by human beings, such as a tool, garment, dwelling, or ornament.

band A territorially based and simply organized group of people who are economically dependent upon hunting and gathering.

B.P. Before the present; years ago.

coiling A method for making pottery by building up the walls of the pot by attaching successive ropelike clay layers, which are then shaped and smoothed to form a seamless vessel.

contact Refers to the first meeting of Indians with the European explorers or settlers; for the Nanticoke and other Middle Atlantic people, contact took place in the early 17th century.

culture The learned behavior of human beings; nonbiological, socially taught activities; the way of life of a given group of people.

culture area A geographic region in which the cultures of a number of tribes or other groups share numerous traits or elements.

environment Natural setting including climate, geographical features, plant and animal life.

family hunting territory An inherited tract of land on which family members have the right to hunt, trap, and fish.

Folsom point A projectile point of shaped stone, found in 1927 near Folsom, New Mexico, in association with bones of the now-extinct *Bison taylori,* and dated to about 10,000 B.P.

habitat The physical aspects of the setting or environment in which a group of humans lives; the geographical features and plant and animal life in the environment. Humans *exploit the habitat* when they draw from it materials necessary for food, clothing, and shelter.

Manito An important deity of the Nanticoke and other Algonkian tribes, considered to be the giver of all good or beneficial things.

marginal environment Region whose resources are inadequate for a group's subsistence needs.

mulatto Person of mixed black and white ancestry.

ossuary A large hole dug in the ground in which bones of the dead are stored or buried.

Paleo-Indian Period The way of life of the first humans in North America, more than 10,000 years ago, during the late Pleistocene (glacial). It involved hunting large mammals and the making of specialized stone tools.

person of color Term used during the 19th century to describe anyone who was not white.

pit house Dwelling of the Archaic Period, constructed by digging a cavity in the earth, lining and covering it with branches or bark.

Pleistocene Geologic period spreading and receding glaciation throughout the earth.

powwow A dance and social gathering held by Nanticoke today, derived in part from similar traditional gatherings of other Indian groups.

prehistoric Anything that happened before written records existed for a given locality. In North America, anything earlier than the first contact with Europeans is considered to be prehistoric; same as pre-contact.

projectile point Stone weapon points purposefully fashioned by human beings.

quiackeson Special ritual structure of the Nanticoke in which the dead were placed for temporary or permanent burial.

reservation A tract of land set aside by the United States or Canadian governments specifically for Indians of a given tribe.

squatters People who occupy land without having legal title to it.

subsistence strategy Ways of acquiring and using available food resources. **Seasonal subsistence strategy** is the planned use of food resources available at different seasons of the year.

tayac Algonquian word meaning the chief or leader.

tenant farming Raising crops on land owned by another person and paying rent in cash or a share of the crops for the right to use the land.

tribe A term used to describe a community or group of several related communities that have a common territory, language, and culture.

trust tribe Those American tribes recognized by the federal government in specific laws and treaties and eligible to receive services from the Bureau of Indian Affairs.

wampum A medium of exchange, or type of money, consisting of beads made from white and purple parts of clam and oyster shells, commonly made and used by Algonkian people. From the Algonquian word *wampumpeaq.*

werowance Algonquian word; a tribal chief.

wigwam A one-room dwelling constructed of a framework of saplings or branches covered with tree bark or woven mats.

Woodland Period The period beginning about 3,000 B.P., characterized in the Middle Atlantic by the beginning of agriculture, pottery making, and permanent villages.

INDEX

ACKNOWLEDGMENTS

Cover: Photograph courtesy of Museum of the American Indian, Heye Foundation.

Pages 12, 16 *bottom*, 46, 49, Maryland Historical Society, Baltimore;   15 *top and bottom*, 16 *left and right*, 34, 60, The Bettmann Archive;   18, 62, 80, 82 *top and bottom*, 91, The A. Aubrey Bodine Collection. The Peale Museum, Baltimore, Maryland;   22 *left and right*, 27, 28 *left*, 29 *right*, 31, Delaware Division of Historical and Cultural Affairs;   28 *right*, 29 *left*, 32, 37, 38, 39, 40, *America 1585: The Complete Drawings of John White*, edited by Paul Hulton. © 1984 University of North Carolina Press. Drawings © 1964 The Trustees of the British Museum. Used with permission of the publisher;   30 *left*, basket in the collection of the Museum of the American Indian, Heye Foundation, photograph by the author;   30 *right*, 50, photographs courtesy of Museum of the American Indian, Heye Foundation;   36, Cary Carson, Historic St. Mary's City;   43, Addison Worthington;   52, 64, 69, 72 *left*, 75, 77, 78, photos by Frank G. Speck. Photographs courtesy of Museum of the American Indian, Heye Foundation;   55 *top*, photo by Carmelo Guadagno. Photograph courtesy of Museum of the American Indian, Heye Foundation;   55 *bottom*, 57 *bottom*, 67, 68, 85, 86, 87, 88, photographs by the author;   57 *top, second, and third rows*, 70, 71, 72 *right*, Frank W. Porter III, Editor, *A Photographic Survey of Indian Mission Church*, 1977;   58, Culver Pictures, Inc.;   59, National Portrait Gallery, Smithsonian Institution, Washington, D.C.; on loan from National Museum of American Art;   81, Delaware Historical Society;   89, 90, courtesy of the Nanticoke Indian Museum.

Maps (frontispiece, pages 20, 21, 44) by Gary Tong.

FRANK W. PORTER III, author of this book and General Editor of this series, is Director of the Chelsea House Foundation for American Indian Studies. He holds an M.A. and Ph.D. from the University of Maryland, where he also earned his B.A. He has done extensive research concerning the Nanticoke and other Indians of Maryland and Delaware, contributing articles on their history, archaeology, geography, and ethnography to numerous publications, and he has produced two documentary films. He was formerly Director of the Maryland Commission on Indian Affairs and American Indian Research and Resource Institute, Gettysburg, Pennsylvania. His work has been supported by grants from the Delaware Humanities Forum, the Maryland Committee for the Humanities, the Ford Foundation, and the National Endowment for the Humanities, among others.

17.95